THE POPE AND THE WITCH

by Dario Fo

Script edited by Franca Rame

Translated by Ed Emery

THE FIRST MIRACLE OF THE BOY JESUS

by Dario Fo

Translated by Ed Emery

OBERON BOOKS
LONDON

This edition first published in Great Britain in 1994 by Oberon Books Limited, 521 Caledonian Road, London N7 9RH
Tel: 0171 607 3637/Fax: 0171 607 3629

Reprinted in this edition by Oberon Books Ltd (incorporating Absolute Classics) in 1997

British Library Cataloguing-in-Publication Data:
A catalogue record for this book is available from the British Library.

ISBN 1 870259 58 0

Cover design: Andrzej Klimowski
Typography: Richard Doust

Printed in Great Britain by Arrowhead Books Ltd, Reading.

CONTENTS

THE POPE AND THE WITCH

Milano – Teatro Lirico, January 1990

THE POPE AND THE WITCH

In the Book of Genesis it says that the first woman was not Eve but Lilith.

A woman who would never accept to be subjected to a man...

She demanded her own complete autonomy, and for this reason she was the first to have to leave Paradise.

I believe that Franca comes from that very particular race of women...

She performs together with me, but she does everything in order not to resemble me in style; she has a style all her own.

She collaborates in the writing of plays, but never in second place.

She won't accept even one line without having discussed it first... She's very insistent!

But it would be a sad day for me if I didn't have this constant stimulus to rewrite, correct, and rework everything again from the beginning... On stage... And with passion.

The text of this play has been edited by Franca.

More than just editing it, France has raised it, brought it up, and made it theatrically readable.

All done with true skill and dedication.

Dario Fo

CHARACTERS

The Pope
First Cardinal: Pope's Personal Secretary
Second Cardinal
Third Cardinal
Professor
First Nun
Second Nun/Healer
Third Nun
Priest in charge of Press Office
Vatican String Quartet
First Young Man
Second Young Man
Third Young Man
First Young Woman/Assistant
Second Young Woman
Third Young Woman
Drunkard
First Gangster
Second Gangster
Small Monk, Poison Tester
Brazilian Nun
Head of the Swiss Guard
Swiss Guards
Total cast list: 13 persons, including doubling-up

ACT ONE

[*We find ourselves in the corridor outside the POPE's apartments in the Vatican.*

The stage is divided by a traverse curtain. On it is painted a large sixteenth-century fresco.

Enter a CARDINAL (the POPE's personal secretary). We hear a warbling sound; the CARDINAL looks about him and raises his cassock circumspectly. From an inside pocket he extracts a mobile telephone, and pulls up the aerial.]

FIRST CARDINAL: Hello... Yes... what's the matter?... I'm right here, outside his rooms... Yes, I know he's late... The trouble is, I don't know whether he's still inside or whether he's gone out already...

[*Enter a NUN. She hurries across the stage.*]

FIRST CARDINAL: [*Trying to stop her.*] Oh, Sister... Just a moment... Sister...?

FIRST NUN: I'll be back in a moment, your Eminence... I have something urgent to see to...

[*She exits, almost running.*]

FIRST CARDINAL: That was the Sister who runs his life... went off like a bat out of hell... no way I could stop her... Well, yes... Maybe he's gone down to take a look at the children... What do you mean, what children? Haven't you seen St Peter's Square this morning...? [*The CAPTAIN OF THE SWISS GUARDS crosses the stage.*] They've been arriving since dawn... Exactly... for the so-called "Gathering of the Innocents"... Of course! I'm the one who does the programming, so obviously I know that he's scheduled to meet them this afternoon... Oh, here's the Sister coming back again... I'll ring off for now. [*He replaces the mobile phone clumsily, forgetting to put down the aerial, which sticks up under his cassock. The FIRST NUN enters, carrying a tray with a jug and a glass on it, all of which is covered with a serviette.*] Oh, Sister... Wait a moment...

FIRST NUN: Yes...? [*She points to his raised cassock.*] Excuse me, your Eminence, what might that be...?!

FIRST CARDINAL: Oh, nothing... Just my aerial...

[*He turns away from the SISTER and fiddles with the aerial in order to get it down.*]

FIRST NUN: Would you like me to give you a hand?

FIRST CARDINAL: No, I can manage, thank you...

[*He gets the aerial down.*]

FIRST NUN: Well, I'm in a terrible hurry, so if you don't mind I must be going.

FIRST CARDINAL: No, wait. I wanted to know what's happened to the Holy Father... Why is he so late this morning?

FIRST NUN: Your Eminence, I'm afraid I really can't...

FIRST CARDINAL: What do you mean, you really can't...! Don't you realise how serious this is...? It's the first time in the history that the head of the Catholic Church has agreed to meet directly with the world's press... journalists from all over the world... And has agreed to answer their questions at a press conference, as if he was some American President... With all the TV channels reporting it live!

FIRST NUN: Yes, I know. But I think we've got a problem on our hands.

FIRST CARDINAL: A problem? You must be joking! Downstairs we've got a hall jam-packed full of journalists... [*He raises the serviette covering the jug and pours himself a drink. The NUN pointlessly tries to stop him.*] What am I going to tell *them*?

[*He downs the drink, and then pours himself another.*]

FIRST NUN: But who would have thought that he'd get all upset over a few children like this?

[*A PRIEST crosses the stage.*]

FIRST CARDINAL: [*Lowering his voice.*] What's so surprising about it? He's always been crazy about children... Kissing babies all over the place...

[*He continues drinking.*]

FIRST NUN: Please, your Eminence, such sarcasm is unbefitting.

FIRST CARDINAL: I'm not being sarcastic... [*He pours himself another drink.*] I'm just saying that this time we're up against a hundred thousand of them... A hundred thousand children, all here in St Peter's Square?! Herod would have had a field day.

FIRST NUN: How can you joke about it, your Eminence... It's terribly serious! He's on the edge of a nervous breakdown. He's started shaking all over.

FIRST CARDINAL: Really? When did this start?

FIRST NUN: About an hour ago.

FIRST CARDINAL: And this is the first you choose to tell me about it? I mean to say, Sister...!

FIRST NUN: Don't blame me – it was the Holy Father. He said: "Don't tell anyone, for goodness sake... With all those journalists around... We mustn't let on... If they ever find out...!"

FIRST CARDINAL: Well, I suppose he's got a point. [*The warbling of a mobile phone again. Another CARDINAL crosses the stage.*] Oh dear, here we go again. Excuse me, Sister... [*The NUN turns slightly, in order not to see the FIRST CARDINAL fumbling under his cassock.*] Hello, who's there...? Hello!

[*The warbling sound continues.*]

SECOND CARDINAL: Oh, it must be mine... [*He pulls a mobile phone out of his sleeve and puts it to his ear.*] Hello... Hello...

FIRST NUN: Ah, actually, it was mine... [*She goes, coyly, to lift her gown.*]

SECOND CARDINAL: When the Day of Judgement comes, the Angels will call us on our mobile phones... And God help anyone who's caught with their batteries flat!

[*He exits.*]

FIRST NUN: [*To the FIRST CARDINAL.*] Would you mind looking the other way? [*She extracts her mobile phone from under her tunic.*] Hello? Yes, it's me. Yes, send them in... Or rather, you'd best bring them in...

[*Both the men put their mobile phones back under their cassocks, remembering to put down their aerials.*]

FIRST CARDINAL: Might I ask who's on their way, Sister?

FIRST NUN: Professor Ridolfi, and one of his assistants.

FIRST CARDINAL: Ridolfi? You mean the psychiatrist?

FIRST NUN: Well, actually he's rather more than just a psychiatrist... He's a neurological surgeon... specialises in nervous disorders.

FIRST CARDINAL: That's what I mean. It seems to me going a bit far to invite someone like that in, just to deal with this childish fixation... I mean... this child fixation...

FIRST NUN: Unfortunately, I really don't think the Holy Father's problem is that simple. Anyway, he was the one who insisted on the Professor being sent for.

FIRST CARDINAL: Ah well, if it was all his idea, fair enough... [*He takes another drink.*] This is good...! What is it?

FIRST NUN: The Holy Father's laxative [*A measured reaction on the part of the CARDINAL.*] Oh, here he comes...

[*Enter the PROFESSOR. He has his doctor's bag with him.*]

FIRST CARDINAL: Ah, Professor... Welcome...!

PROFESSOR: I was held up by your Guards... They insisted on putting me through a metal detector... They even took away my little hammer for testing reflexes...

FIRST CARDINAL: After all that hoo-ha in Panama they've become rather over-keen... But where's your assistant?

PROFESSOR: I was just wondering that myself. I think she must have got lost down a corridor somewhere...

[*Enter the PROFESSOR's assistant: the SECOND NUN. She carries two large bags, and an African bow.*]

SECOND NUN: Here I am.. Here I am... I was held up by two Swiss Guards. They wouldn't let me pass, on account of this sacred bow and arrows, which is an extra-special present for the Pope. They blunted all my arrows, and pulled out all my feathers... of the arrows, I mean... And then they insisted that I put little stickers on the rude bits of these naked men. [*She points to the bow.*] I didn't have any! So I stuck some stamps on instead... Vatican Christmas stamps!

FIRST CARDINAL: I know... bit of a problem, our security services... They're a bit edgy, these days... Anyway, I'm delighted to see you. I'm sure that you'll have everything sorted out in no time... My problem is that downstairs we've got a hall full of journalists waiting. How long is all this going to take?

PROFESSOR: How can I say, your Eminence? I still don't know what the problem is... At least give me a moment...

FIRST CARDINAL: Yes, yes, take as much time as you need. Anyway, maybe I might venture a guess... In my humble opinion, I would say it's just hypertension due to a state of stress.

PROFESSOR: Let's hope that you're right.

FIRST CARDINAL: Follow me. I'll lead the way.

PROFESSOR: No, please, your Eminence. I prefer to see the patient in private... I'm sure you understand.

FIRST CARDINAL: Certainly... fine... no problem...

PROFESSOR: Good... [*To the SECOND NUN, his assistant.*] Right, Sister, this way, let's go...

FIRST CARDINAL: Let's hope you come up with something, Professor... I'll be waiting outside...

PROFESSOR: Relax, Cardinal, relax...

[*The traverse curtain with the painted fresco rises. We find ourselves in a large room with many columns. There are four windows down one wall of the room, stage-left, which divides at an angle; backstage right hangs a large curtain. There is nobody on stage.*]

PROFESSOR: Your Holiness...? Hello... Are you there, your Holiness...?

[*From behind the curtain a dummy appears. It is a perfect reproduction of the POPE. At the same time the POPE himself peers out from the opposite side.*]

POPE: Here I am... And who might you be?

PROFESSOR: What do you mean, who might I be...? I thought it was you who sent for me!

POPE: Ah, you must be the Professor... [*At this moment the POPE emerges from the other end of the curtain.*] At last! Welcome, Professor!

PROFESSOR: This is extraordinary! A double Pope?!

POPE: [*He emerges fully from behind the curtain, and brings the mobile dummy forward with him.*] Well, of course, this one's only a dummy... Tell me what you think – it's a good likeness, isn't it! It was given to me by a Sicilian wood-carver, one of those who make puppets... You know... [*He laughs, amused.*] Ha, ha... A puppet-Pope. Amusing, eh?

PROFESSOR: [*Worried.*] Are you feeling alright, your Holiness?

POPE: Yes. [*He points to the SECOND NUN accompanying the PROFESSOR.*] Who is this Sister? Is she with you...? Does she have to be here? [*The phone rings. He picks it up.*] Hello? [*We hear a din coming from the phone, the sound of loud rock music.*] Who's there? Who? Panama...? The Papal legation? What on earth is that racket...? The US marines again...? What do they want...? Manuel Noriega? But I thought we just handed him over...? He's come back? So how did he manage to get back in...? In a lorry full of pineapples...!! Send him back to the Americans at once! [*He puts down the phone.*] That Noriega... Ever since he heard someone say that religion was the opium of the people, he won't leave us alone for a minute! Anyway, as I was saying, who is this Sister? What's she doing here...?

PROFESSOR: She is my assistant and one of my most valued colleagues... You need have no worries about her... Now, tell me...

POPE: On the contrary, I *am* worried... Because I think I know that face from somewhere... I would like to see her bare-headed, if you don't mind...

PROFESSOR: Bareheaded? Why?

POPE: I don't think she's really a nun at all.

PROFESSOR: Oh, really! You're beginning to worry me, your Holiness. What's got into you? What is this paranoia? [*Addressing the FIRST NUN, the POPE's housekeeper.*] Maybe he's worse than we feared.

POPE: Ah, there! So *you* think I'm mad too, eh?!

PROFESSOR: Who thinks you're mad...?

[*From offstage we hear the sound of children's voices.*]

POPE: Shush! What's all that shouting...? It must be more children arriving in the Square..? Shut all the windows!

[*The FIRST NUN hurries over, assisted by the SECOND NUN, and closes the windows. The sound of voices stops.*]

PROFESSOR: There, that's what I mean. What is this I've been hearing about you locking yourself in your room because you're terrified of children?

POPE: Yes, it's true... [*He points to the window.*] Look, every time I look out, there are more of them... But it's not so much them and their shouting that worries me... I'm more worried about the trap that they're organising for me...

PROFESSOR: What trap...? And *who's* organising?

POPE: [*Looking around cautiously.*] There's a plot.

PROFESSOR: A plot? What sort of plot?

POPE: Can't you even guess?

SECOND NUN: If you don't mind me interrupting, I think I know what his Holiness means.

POPE: Let's see if you're shrewder than the Professor here.

SECOND NUN: Well, to start with, as I was coming across the Square, I stopped to take a look for a moment, and I noticed that most of these children are mixed-race and mulattoes from South America... and Filippinos... and little black children...

POPE: Well done... Spot on...! In other words, all children from the Third World...

SECOND NUN: Yes. Then I asked around, and I discovered that almost all of them are orphans... No parents...

POPE: Exactly... My compliments! Sit down.

PROFESSOR: Why compliments..? What are you getting at?

POPE: Come on, Professor... Make an effort... Use your imagination. In your opinion, who was it brought all these children together and organised all the transport to bring them to Rome?

SECOND NUN: If I might assist you, Professor, I'd say that here we're dealing with an organisation that is very powerful, and which has considerable financial resources.

POPE: Exactly! How did you guess?

PROFESSOR: Well it's hardly a secret, is it, seeing it's been in all the papers... They've been organised by the IMPAC, the International Movement for the Protection of Abandoned Children.

POPE: And to what end has this so-called "IMPAC" taken on the rather expensive task of bringing all these children to Rome?

PROFESSOR: Well, I presume they've come for the same reason that brings millions of Christians to Rome every year. They want to see the Pope in person, and they want to receive your blessing.

POPE: Oh yes? So there they are, all these poor little orphans, in Africa, Brazil, Colombia and India and so on... And all of a sudden they feel this irresistible urge: "I want to see the Pope... Bump-di-dum... I want the Pope... Bump-di-dum!"

SECOND NUN: Ooh, you've got a lovely sense of humour, your Holiness, really.

POPE: Thank you... I suppose you think I'm a bit eccentric...

SECOND NUN: Incidentally, I talked to some of the children from Zambia, and when they found out that I was coming to see you, they asked me to bring you this bow... It's a sacred bow.

[*She hands him the bow.*]

POPE: How lovely! All these little men, all these lovely little authority figures, all piled up, one on top of the other, according to their rank... Imagine if we did this sort of thing in the Vatican! You'd have me, going round with all these cardinals on my head... Mind you, I wouldn't fancy having Poletti on my head!

PROFESSOR: You see? It's a gesture of affection, Your Holiness, if I were you I wouldn't worry so much... Obviously, the people who brought all these children together thought it would be a wonderful thing if thousands of poor children from all around the world could enjoy this extraordinary privilege.

POPE: Oh yes? And now you tell me that *I'm* the mad one, the eccentric one?

[*The SECOND NUN hands the bow to the FIRST NUN, who leans it against a wall.*]

PROFESSOR: I don't understand... Are you saying that *I'm* mad?

SECOND NUN: Well really, Professor, hasn't it even occurred to you that these so-called protectors of abandoned infants might actually be bogus...? Am I right, Your Holiness?

POPE: Absolutely, absolutely.

SECOND NUN: An organisation cunningly concealing itself behind this apparently humanitarian venture... with who knows what vile purposes.

POPE: Oh, finally, someone who knows what they're talking about! You've hit the nail on the head!

PROFESSOR: Whereas I, on the other hand, am some kind of congenital idiot? Alright. If these people aren't from the organisation that they claim to belong to, then who are they?

POPE: Nothing more nor less than a movement of fanatical birth control activists, who are in favour of the totally free distribution of contraceptives and prophylactics.

SECOND NUN: I wouldn't be at all surprise if the sponsors of this plot turned out to be the big American manufacturers of surgical goods and rubberware...

POPE: Ah yes, surgical goods and rubberware... I hadn't thought of that... My compliments, Sister!

PROFESSOR: Excuse me, but if you ask me this is verging on paranoia... You in particular, Sister.

POPE: Oh yes? So I suppose the security services of the pontifical state are also verging on paranoia, when they send me these security despatches?

[*He picks up a big dossier and passes it to the SECOND NUN.*]

PROFESSOR: Why, what do they say?

POPE: I am kept up to date, on an hourly basis, on all the movements of these provocateurs extraordinaires; to such an extent that I am now in a position to be able to give you a fair idea of what will happen at the precise moment when I appear on the balcony.

PROFESSOR: So what's going to happen, then?

POPE: At that very moment they will release hundreds of banners, with messages in all different languages... and at the same time, over a very powerful loudhailer system, they will start shouting: "Here you are, Holy Father, you ordered us to love one another, and to go forth and multiply... iply... iply..." There'll be an echo, you see. "Bring forth many children of God into the light of day... Who cares if then they all die like flies!"

PROFESSOR: [*Shocked.*] No!

FIRST NUN: They'll really say that?!

POPE: Yes. "Who cares if then they all die of hunger at the rate of thirty-five million a year... if half of them end up abandoned, forty-eight million of them in five years alone... or if they end up illiterate, imprisoned, half starved, exploited and wretched for the rest of their lives. What matters is that they be brought into the world, because life is sacred, even though their life is disgusting... ting... ting..."

SECOND NUN: Quite right.

POPE: What?!

SECOND NUN: I mean, yes, that's exactly what they'll say. [*She is embarrassed, and in an attempt to overcome her gaffe she waves the documents in her hand.*] It's written here, in the despatches.

PROFESSOR: Incredible...! But surely, won't the police be able to stop them and seize their public address system...?

POPE: Yes, but at that moment their master plan goes into action. They'll send up an enormous banner, suspended from hundreds of balloons. [*He points to one of the windows.*] Look, you can see the balloons down there, all ready... It will rise slowly into the sky over Rome... And it'll be readable from every part of the city.

PROFESSOR: Is this spelled out in the despatches too?

POPE: Yes, yes, look... Word for word...

[*He passes him some sheets of paper.*]

PROFESSOR: And what will be written on this enormous banner?

POPE: [*He seizes some sheets from the SECOND NUN's hand.*] "Holy Father, you wanted all these children. It was you who said: 'Suffer the little children to come unto me!' Well here they are! [*He throws all the papers in the air.*] They're all yours! Take them, *you* bring them up!" And they'll dump them all right here. You see? A hundred thousand children, here, in St Peter's Square... all crying... and shouting... and bawling... and hungry... And what am *I* supposed to do with them? Where am I supposed to put them? A hundred thousand children! With all the hotels and convents and Catholic youth hostels all full up for the World Cup?

[*The two NUNS gather up the sheets of paper.*]

PROFESSOR: But how can they! It's criminal! After bringing them all the way here, they just dump them... without anyone to look after them? It's scandalous...! What a shitty trick... It's bloody obscene... [*He breaks off, embarrassed.*] Oh, I'm sorry...

POPE: I can think of no more fitting words to define the revolting situation in which I shall find myself!

PROFESSOR: But seeing that you already know what's going to happen, why don't you just arrest them now?

POPE: Oh yes? And what would we charge them with? You need proof to arrest people, but by the time we have the proof it will be too late. By then they'll have made a mockery of me and of the Church as a whole. Can you imagine the scandal! The laughter...! What a disaster!

SECOND NUN: [*Aside, to the PROFESSOR.*] If you ask me, as of this moment, if a child comes anywhere near him, he'd eat it alive.

POPE: So at this point I think you'll agree that I've got good reason to be apprehensive, Professor!

PROFESSOR: Certainly, certainly. Very good reason.

[*The FIRST CARDINAL puts his head round the door, rather nervously.*]

FIRST CARDINAL: Excuse me, may I...

POPE: Who's that? I'm not seeing anyone!

PROFESSOR: It's only your personal secretary.

POPE: I'm sorry... I saw red. What do you want?

FIRST CARDINAL: I'm worried, Holy Father...

POPE: You have good reason to be... You drank my laxative...! No, I'm only joking. I know: you're worried about all those journalists downstairs. I'm not coming down, though! I'm sorry, but I am physically and psychologically quite incapable of meeting with them. Isn't that right, Professor?

PROFESSOR: Absolutely... It would be quite inappropriate.

FIRST CARDINAL: I understand, but it's not the journalists I'm worrying about, your Holiness... I've already told them that the press conference is being postponed... I'm worried about the children... You know... The "Gathering of the Innocents". The square is filling up a lot faster than expected... The two shipfuls of children arrived in port earlier than they were supposed to...

FIRST NUN: [*Going over to the window.*] Look at all those coaches!

FIRST CARDINAL: They've been there for half an hour now, and many of the rest have been here since dawn. In my opinion, your Holiness, you should bring forward the time of your meeting with the poor things.

POPE: In other words, you want me to go out on the balcony *now*... with my arms outstretched towards all the children... instead of waiting till the afternoon?

FIRST CARDINAL: Yes... Poor things, they're starting to show signs of tiredness and restlessness... Look, they're all so jammed in together!

FIRST NUN: [*Going across to one of the windows.*] Heaven's above, what a crowd! I've never seen so many children all in one place!

POPE: [*Barely peeking out of the window, and suddenly drawing back.*] Yes, they really are an incredible number!

SECOND NUN: Look at them all! You know what – they remind me of the story of Little Pea...

POPE: Little Pea?

SECOND NUN: Don't you know the story, your Holiness?

POPE: No.

SECOND NUN: Would you like me to tell it to you?

FIRST CARDINAL: This is hardly the right moment for stories about Little Pea!

POPE: A Pope should know all stories... seeing that that is what Popes do, tell stories... How does it go? Come and sit down.

SECOND NUN: You know, the story about the mother who was so desperate to have children that she went to see a wizard...

POPE: No, I don't remember it... What does the wizard do?

SECOND NUN: Well, there was once this woman. She really, really wanted to have children, but unfortunately for her, her husband had taken a vow of total chastity.

POPE: [*To the FIRST CARDINAL.*] We're giving that Formigoni too much leeway!

SECOND NUN: She despairs. She cries from morning to night. She wails... "I shall never be a mother! I shall never be a mother!" She shouts it out of the window too: "I shall never be a mother!" All of a sudden a gynaecologist passes by. He happened to be out jogging, with the word "Gynaecologist" written across his track suit top... Backwards, like they do with ambulances... And he says: "We could make you a couple of babies in a test tube." "Babies in a test tube? No, never! It would be a sin!" "Well alright then, with frozen eggs." "Frozen eggs?!" "Only the best free-range, of course!" "Get thee behind me, Satan!"

POPE: Well said!

SECOND NUN: Thank you. So, in desperation the woman goes to see a wizard, a holy man who lived in a hermitage on a working-class housing estate. "Listen to me, Woman, your faith will be rewarded. You want children? Well then, go home and put a handful of beans on to boil. Black-eye beans. Don't use frozen beans, because they're contrary to nature and they might turn out freaks. Put these freaks... I mean, these black-eyed beans... on to boil and just when they come to the boil, throw them onto the floor... And you will see, you'll get two or three beautiful children, with a black eye... I mean, with two black eyes." No sooner said than done! The women goes home, puts water on the stove, and, seeing that she's so greedy for children, she throws in half a sack of these black-eye beans... and she stirred... and stirred... "I don't want them to stick... I don't want to end up with Siamese twins..." she shouted. As it came to the boil... Crash, she hurled this great beanery to the floor, and... Ping... Pong... Ping... Pong... Hey presto! From every bean a child was born... Two... three... seven... nine babies! "I'm a

mother, I'm a mother," she shouted, happily... Twelve, eighteen, twenty-one... "I'm a mother!" Thirty-seven, forty-nine, eighty-three, ninety-five, ninety-seven... one hundred... One hundred babies! "I'm a mother..." She was starting to get a bit worried. "I'm a mother..."
A hundred babies, all with these bright little black eyes, leaping around, jumping up and down, arguing, and growing... By the end of ten seconds they already had long hair down to here... four sharp little teeth, hard nails... And they started shouting that they were hungry, because children who are born from beans can speak as soon as they're born. They started gobbling up everything in sight, including all the furniture in the house, and then they started attacking the mother... Her legs, her bottom, her breasts... it was incredible! They swarmed all over her, chewing bits off her, biting her neck, taking lumps out of her ears... They were incredibly fast eaters, you see. The poor woman was desperate, and in order to save herself she grabbed a frying pan... and squish-squish-squish, she started bashing all her little bean babies. What a terrible sight! All her children squashed! Out of all this terrible massacre, only one little child was saved – and he wasn't a bean at all, he was a pea. A tiny little green pea child. He'd managed to save himself by hiding in a thimble. "But how is it that you are so small?" the women asked. "I wath not born from a bean," said the pea, "but from a dried pea, which jutht happened to end up in that bag." "Ah, so that's why you're so green... Poor Little Pea!" "Don't make fun of me! I know I'm green, and I know you find me repellent... Thquash me, thquash me! Take your frying pan and thquash me!'" (Children born from green peas all have this kind of lisp.) "No," says the woman, hugging the child to her breast. "I shall love you and care for you always. It doesn't matter if you're green... You'll see, soon you'll find other greens like yourself, and together you'll all set up a lovely big ecology party."

POPE: The story has a certain moral... We had a story like that where I come from, a Slavic story, except that when we told it, it was dried chestnuts... And instead of peas, we used a chickpea, which went on to found the Solidarity movement in Poland. I'm joking... I made it up...!

So where is the moral? Am I supposed to be the mother, because first I encourage the birth of children and then I end up being terrified of them?

SECOND NUN: I hope you won't be offended, your Holiness, but, for me, yes, I suppose you are a kind of big mother.

POPE: A big mother!! Listen, Sister, you might recall what happened to my predecessor in this job, when he proclaimed that God was more mother than father... It seems that the Good Lord rather took offence at this, and decided to call him to meet his Maker rather earlier than expected... But this is the first time I've heard anyone calling the Pope a "big mother". Is this a provocation, or are you trying to...

[*From offstage the sound of children's voices becomes louder. The POPE breaks off.*]

FIRST CARDINAL: [*Looking out of the window.*] Holy Mother, what a pandemonium!

POPE: "Holy Mother"? You see – now see what you've started!

FIRST CARDINAL: They'll cause a riot at this rate!

PROFESSOR: There are more groups arriving too... Your Holiness, come and see... It's an amazing sight!

POPE: [*He sits down.*] No thank you, I'll take your word for it.

SECOND NUN: Holy Father... something seems to be happening to your eyes...

POPE: My eyes?

SECOND NUN: They're getting all red and watery...
Look, professor...

PROFESSOR: Looks like an inflammation to me...

SECOND NUN: If you'll allow me... I've got just the very
thing.

[*She takes a small bottle of eye drops from her handbag.*]

POPE: That's very kind of you, but...

[*The SECOND NUN more or less forces his head back.*]

SECOND NUN: Keep still... Look up... Look towards
me... No, don't shut your eyes...

[*She drops a couple of drops from the dropper into the
POPE'S eyes.*]

FIRST CARDINAL: I think it would be appropriate, your
Holiness, if you went out onto the balcony. Just for a
moment... to say a few words of welcome...

POPE: No, for goodness sake... That would be the signal
for the loudhailers and the posters...

FIRST CARDINAL: [*Not understanding.*] Loudhailers and
posters?

POPE: This is very strange... I'm feeling all dizzy...

SECOND NUN: Try looking at my hand... Can you see it?

POPE: Yes. It looks rather peculiar, though. Distorted,
crooked, somehow...

SECOND NUN: Come over here... [*She helps the POPE
up, and leads him to one of the windows.*] Try walking a
bit... Can you see better now?

POPE: [*Approaching cautiously.*] Yes, that's better... But
what are those children doing down there? They seem
to be climbing up.

FIRST CARDINAL: Where? I don't see anyone climbing up.

POPE: What are you, blind as well as stupid? Look, there!

FIRST CARDINAL: I don't see anything...

SECOND NUN: There, coming up the columns. Look, one of them's fallen!

POPE: Two, in fact...! But the others are still climbing... Heavens, they're terribly brave!

SECOND NUN: Of course they are...! Seeing these kids have been out on the streets virtually since the day they were born, they're absolutely fearless!

POPE: And they're violent too... Look, they've attacked that group of priests who were trying to block their way...

FIRST NUN: Oh! They're hitting the priests!

SECOND NUN: And biting the nuns!

FIRST CARDINAL: But where? I don't see them... I can't see a thing!

FIRST NUN: Me neither!

PROFESSOR: Down there... They're rushing about like headless chickens on a battery farm.

FIRST CARDINAL: Chickens too, now! That's incredible! But where?

POPE: Coming up the front there. It's incredible! They're climbing up the front of St Peter's... They're climbing up by hanging onto balloons!

[*Through the window we see clusters of balloons floating up.*]

FIRST CARDINAL: Chickens hanging from balloons? I see no chickens... [*The SECOND NUN stamps on his foot.*] Ouch! What was that for, Sister?!

SECOND NUN: Stand more over that way. Surely you can see them now, loads of children hanging onto clusters of balloons and being carried up by them? Quick! We'd better burst their balloons before they get a grip on the window sill...

PROFESSOR: What with, though?

POPE: We could burst them with those halberds.

[*He points to halberds hanging on the wall. The PROFESSOR and the SECOND NUN take them, and move across to the window.*]

SECOND NUN: Mind we don't puncture ourselves too, eh!

POPE: And pass me the sacred bow from Zambia.

[*The FIRST NUN passes him the bow.*]

PROFESSOR: That's the way! Lay on, Macduff! And you too, Cardinal. See if you can find something to throw.

[*The FIRST CARDINAL takes two silver-gilt apples from a bowl. After examining them to see if they're valuable, he shrugs his shoulders and throws them.*]

SECOND NUN: There, I hit one! I knocked him down!

FIRST CARDINAL: Where?

PROFESSOR: There... Two balloons, with a child hanging underneath! [*He makes a gesture as if bursting the balloon.*] Take that...! That's dealt with that one!

FIRST NUN: Watch out, over there... one of the balloons has come in the window... Oh, it's alright – it didn't have a child on it...

PROFESSOR: Uh oh – trouble! One of the kids just got in through that window over there!

SECOND NUN: And he's hidden behind the curtain at the back!

POPE: Stop him, catch him!

PROFESSOR: [*He runs behind the curtain. The SECOND NUN follows him, carrying her big handbag.*] Aha! Got you! It's alright – I've caught him...!

[*The curtain shakes as if a struggle is taking place behind it.*

We catch a glimpse of a child's head. This is a doll, which the SECOND NUN had in her handbag, together with the dagger which the PROFESSOR is wielding.]

SECOND NUN: Watch out, he's got a knife!

PROFESSOR: [*Yelling.*] Ooooh! Ouch!

SECOND NUN: What happened?

[*The PROFESSOR comes from behind the curtain with a dagger sticking in his chest.*]

PROFESSOR: He stabbed me...

POPE: Oh, my God!

[*The child-doll flies into the air above the curtain. The POPE fires an arrow at it. With some co-ordination, he may succeed in hitting it.*]

SECOND NUN: There, take that, you brat! [*We hear the crash of breaking glass.*] Whew, at last! [*She comes back on stage.*] I threw him out of the window.

POPE: Oh, how terrible! Oh, the poor thing!

[*The POPE also runs behind the curtain.*]

FIRST CARDINAL: [*To the PROFESSOR.*] Are you alright, Professor?

PROFESSOR: Yes, yes... It's nothing... Just a scratch... [*He pulls the dagger out of his chest, and looks at it.*] ...about three inches deep...! I'm dying!

[*He falls backwards on the floor.*]

[*The POPE re-enters.*]

POPE: I think I shot down one of the children with an arrow.

[*He goes back behind the curtain.*]

FIRST CARDINAL: I think I'm going crazy...! Were you really dying just then, Professor...?

PROFESSOR: [*Confidentially, to FIRST CARDINAL.*] Don't be silly – we're acting... It's a role-playing routine. We're helping the Holy Father to act out his fears, as a way of getting him over his phobias.

FIRST CARDINAL: Oh, I see... So we're supposed to play along with him!

PROFESSOR: Well done! So now you can give a hand too!

FIRST CARDINAL: [*He takes the PROFESSOR's dagger, runs to the window, and mimes a big battle.*] OK, come on, let's be having you! Take that! That's sorted you out... scumbag! Ha!

[*The POPE re-enters.*]

POPE: What on earth do you think you're doing, Cardinal?

FIRST CARDINAL: I've just polished off one of those evil Satanic children!

POPE: And I suppose you're happy now... I suppose that makes you feel good? The poor thing...

FIRST CARDINAL: It was legitimate self-defence.

POPE: Legitimate self-defence? Against a poor, starving little mixed-race kiddie! You're a monster!

FIRST CARDINAL: What do you mean? You throw them out of the window, and shoot them full of arrows, and then *I'm* the monster!?

SECOND NUN: Ah yes – but then we feel terrible about it afterwards. We find it repugnant... But you're obviously getting a kick out of it! If you ask me, you're a sadist!

FIRST CARDINAL: No, no, I felt terrible about it too.

POPE: Silence, hypocrite!

[*He fires an arrow at the CARDINAL. It bounces off his stomach.*]

FIRST CARDINAL: Your Holiness! That's no way to treat a Cardinal!

POPE: Forgive me, but beneath these robes beats the heart of an actor who can't stand the sight of priests... Faced with a Cardinal, I don't know how to restrain myself. [*He goes back into character as the POPE.*] Oh... it's over... at last!

[*He settles into a chair and closes his eyes, as if sleeping.*]

FIRST NUN: Amazing – look, all the children are starting to leave the square.

PROFESSOR: Yes, they're loading them back on the buses... They're going away.

FIRST CARDINAL: I don't see what's so amazing about that! Seeing that the Pope shows no signs of appearing on the balcony, they're taking them off to get something to eat. It's all part of the programme...

SECOND NUN: [*To the FIRST CARDINAL, stamping on his foot again.*] Shush!

FIRST CARDINAL: Ouch!

SECOND NUN: [*She goes over to the POPE and waves her hand slowly in front of his eyes.*] Hooray! We did it! It's all over now, your Holiness!

FIRST CARDINAL: [*Limping.*] Sister, are you out of your mind? Now you've crushed my other foot! Why didn't I just stick to being parish priest in Bassano del Grappa!?

POPE: [*Waking up again.*] What's all the shouting about? What's going on? Oh, I must have nodded off... I'm sorry... [*He sees SECOND NUN.*] Who's the Sister? Oh yes, now I remember... She's the Sister with the excellent intuition. [*To PROFESSOR.*] Professor...? What on earth are you doing here? Oh, how silly of me... It was me who asked you to come, wasn't it... I wasn't feeling very well, you know... Because what happened was that... Oh, I don't remember now... Anyway, it'll come back to me... Goodness, I'm late... [*To FIRST CARDINAL.*] Cardinal, what about the journalists?

FIRST CARDINAL: Oh, for heaven's sake...

POPE: For heaven's sake what?

FIRST CARDINAL: For heaven's sake maybe I'll be in time to stop them.

POPE: Tell them that I'll be ready to meet them in fifteen minutes. [*Turning to the FIRST NUN.*] Sister, call my valet to come and give me a hand, because I have to change.

FIRST CARDINAL: But, your Holiness...

POPE: Don't go away, Professor, I'll be back in a minute... I must say, I'm feeling rather peculiar...

[*He exits in a hurry, followed by the FIRST NUN.*]

FIRST CARDINAL: It's incredible! It's as if he doesn't remember a thing. What's come over him?

SECOND NUN: What's come over him is that I brought him out of the trance... So now all he has is a few half-memories.

FIRST CARDINAL: [*Shocked.*] Trance? What trance? When did he go into a trance... And who put him into it?

PROFESSOR: You remember when she went to put the ointment into his eyes...? Well, she was really just pretending... In actual fact, by waving her hands in front of his eyes she was able to guide him from a state of paranoid hysteria into a controlled trance. Fortunately for us the Sister has considerable powers of exorcism.

SECOND NUN: Pleased to meet you. Would you care to avail yourself of my services too? We could do a group discount.

FIRST CARDINAL: You exorcised his Holiness? On whose authority, may I ask...? This is appalling?

PROFESSOR: But don't you realise, we freed him from a nightmare that could have led him to a total breakdown?

FIRST CARDINAL: Well, I'm lost for words... You'll have to excuse me. Lord, what a day! You may have freed the Holy Father, but now *I'm* the one heading for a nervous breakdown! Anyway, even though I don't agree with your methods, thank you, Sister.

SECOND NUN: Don't mention it.

FIRST CARDINAL: [*Picking up the POPE's "despatches".*] And what about these...? Look! These were supposed to be special security bulletins... but there's no mention of a plot anywhere here...

PROFESSOR: Hardly surprising. They're Met Office reports!

FIRST CARDINAL: [*He reads.*] "Winds light to variable... Maximum temperature fifteen degrees Celsius." So the Holy Father was only pretending to read... In actual fact he was making it all up?

PROFESSOR: No, not at all. He actually *believed* he was reading them... It was all going on in his subconscious.

SECOND NUN: There! Now just imagine if he'd gone down to meet the journalists in a frame of mind like that... waving the sacred bow... and saying: "I handed over Noriega to the Americans. They've promised me they won't sentence him to death. Instead they'll punish him by making him write a hundred lines a day: 'No cocaine! Cocaine is bad for you! No cocaine! Cocaine is bad for you!'"

FIRST CARDINAL: But do you really think that the Holy Father is going mad?

PROFESSOR: No, not mad... He is in a highly excitable state, though.

FIRST CARDINAL: So what do you suggest we do about it?

PROFESSOR: He'll need a course of treatment.

SECOND NUN: That's right – complete rest and relaxation..

FIRST CARDINAL: Rest and relaxation? A rest cure! Easier said than done, for a Pope...!

SECOND NUN: [*She rummages in her bag and pulls out a cigarette.*] Exactly. The only real cure would be to give up being Pope.

FIRST CARDINAL: We'd have to sack him. You can't do that! You can't sack a Pope!

SECOND NUN: Why not? You got rid of the last one quick enough, John Paul the First, when he started raving round like a loony and telling Pinocchio stories... talking about breaking up the IOR, you certainly got rid of *him*!

FIRST CARDINAL: Sister, I will not permit you to make gratuitous and poisonous insinuations.... John Paul the First died from natural causes.

SECOND NUN: Well, seeing that natural causes seemed to work so well last time, maybe we could try them again. Mind you, it'd be a shame, really, because I've taken a bit of a liking to this Pope.

[*She lights her cigarette.*]

FIRST CARDINAL: That's quite enough, Sister... Don't you dare use language like that! [*He realises that she is smoking.*] You're smoking?!

SECOND NUN: [*Caught on the hop.*] ...It helps my asthma.

FIRST CARDINAL: [*To the PROFESSOR.*] Professor, where in heaven's name did you find this Sister? She's very strange.

PROFESSOR: You'll have to make allowances for her. She's a missionary... unaccustomed to our worldly ways. I met her in Africa, when I was on a secondment in Burundi. She was running a leprosy colony; then she took up curing people who believed they'd been possessed by demons; and then people with the plague...

SECOND NUN: That was the life!

FIRST CARDINAL: Well, that explains where she acquired her curiously... uncivilised habits... Like some Bantu witch!

SECOND NUN: Watch who you're calling a witch, Cardinal, or I might just turn nasty. I'll turn you into a baboon, and you can wear your little red bobble hat on your baldy backside!

FIRST CARDINAL: Don't talk to me like that, Sister! You're very lucky that you're under the protection of the Professor! I think it's high time you were leaving. Right?!

SECOND NUN: Nothing could give me greater pleasure! [*She picks up her bags.*] I shall go back to my drug addicts. At least they show a bit of gratitude... Not like some people I could name...

FIRST CARDINAL: Drug addicts? What's all this about drug addicts?

PROFESSOR: Well, actually, this likeable good Samaritan runs a centre for the rehabilitation and cure of drug addicts and social misfits.

SECOND NUN: That's right. We work wonders there.

PROFESSOR: Let's say a charitable institution which is not exactly registered with the authorities...

SECOND NUN: The Council were just on the point of shutting me down. The Professor took advantage of this fact to do a bit of blackmail on me.

PROFESSOR: I wouldn't exactly call it blackmail...

SECOND NUN: That's what I said – blackmail. He came to visit me, and more or less told me: "Listen, I can save you. I can stop them evicting you, you and your drug centre and throwing you all out in the street like they did the Leoncavallo centre... I can also help you to escape a prison sentence for serious professional misconduct... In exchange, however, I want you to do me a favour. The Pope is sick. I want you to come to the Vatican with me and see if you can use your hypnosis to cure him. Take it or leave it."

FIRST CARDINAL: But you must be out of your mind, Professor. You bring a person here, who has been involved in illegal acts, who is operating outside the law, and you put the Holy Father in her hands! Supposing people got to hear of it!?

PROFESSOR: How many times do I have to tell you – unorthodox situations require unorthodox remedies.

SECOND NUN: Forget it, Professor. I can't say I've got a lot of time for his Eminence... The man's got no style... [*She looks around for an ashtray. She doesn't find one, so she passes her cigarette stub to the CARDINAL.*] I wouldn't want to desecrate the Holy See... Anyway, his Eminence is right... As Cardinal Biffi put it so nicely, we women are dismal creatures... advisors of the Devil, and propagators of death! The best thing we can do is just pull the chain and disappear from history. Goodbye.

[*She heads for the exit; the PROFESSOR follows.*]

[*Enter the POPE, followed by FIRST NUN. SECOND NUN and the PROFESSOR are stopped in their tracks.*]

POPE: Here I am. Right, your Eminence, are we ready...? [*He sees the cigarette in the FIRST CARDINAL's hand.*] Smoking, your Eminence?!

FIRST CARDINAL: [*Extremely embarrassed.*] Um, er... it helps my asthma.

[*He passes the cigarette stub to the FIRST NUN, who goes to stub it out.*]

POPE: Shame on you! [*He points to the PROFESSOR's briefcase, and then takes it from him.*] Oh, at last! Wonderful! You've found Calvi's briefcase! All this time we've been looking for it...!

PROFESSOR: No, no, your Holiness... That's *my* case...

POPE: Oh what a shame, I suppose we'll never find it now. [*He gives it back to him.*] Now, let's get organised. [*To the FIRST CARDINAL.*] Your Eminence, before we go down, wouldn't it be an idea if you gave me a preview of some of the questions that they're going to be asking?

FIRST CARDINAL: Ah, exactly – just what I was about to propose.

[*He pulls out his mobile phone.*]

POPE: [*To the PROFESSOR and the SECOND NUN.*] You know, sometimes these journalists are so poisonous in their interviews that if a person doesn't turn up well prepared... I tell you what, do me a favour, I'd like you to stay as well... It'll be educational.

[*A young PRIEST appears on stage, holding a folder full of papers. He is the Vatican Press Officer.*]

PRIEST: Excuse me, your Holiness...

FIRST CARDINAL: Ah, there you are, I was just about to come looking for you.

POPE: Who's he?

FIRST CARDINAL: He's the new attache at the Vatican Press Office.

POPE: [*To the PRIEST.*] Oh, good... do sit down... This gives us a bit of time to prepare ourselves...

FIRST NUN: Your Holiness, the musicians are outside, the ones you asked for... Do you want them to come back later?

POPE: No, no, bring them in. [*The FIRST NUN ushers in the string quartet, which consists of two NUNS and two young PRIESTS.*] Set yourselves up over there, and let's have something nice and soothing... It'll help me to think... [*The quartet sets itself up in a corner of the salon, and performs an eighteenth-century largo. The POPE turns to the PRIEST.*] Right, fire away.

PRIEST: Well, the correspondent of the London Daily Express wants to know your reactions to the statement made by the Bishop of Cologne, Gruber Kutter, when he said, and I quote: "I find it ridiculous that, on the threshold of the year 2000, Catholics are still tearing themselves apart over the question of contraception..." [*The STRING QUARTET breaks off for a moment.*] Yes, that's exactly what he says... "of contraception, of the pill, of the coil... of the..."

POPE: Alright, alright, you don't have to list them all!

[*The STRING QUARTET begins playing again.*]

PRIEST: I'm sorry... Anyway, he carries on: "It's no business of the Pope to be handing down instructions about contraceptives. These are not matters to be laid down and dictated by the Church. It is not the Church's business."

POPE: So it's not our business, eh? Well, you can tell Gruber Kutter that the next time there's a Vatican Council I shall find him a nice little parish in Upper Bavaria. With the goats.

[*The STRING QUARTET breaks off again.*]

SECOND NUN: Which, as we know, are not noted for their use of prophylactics.

PROFESSOR: Calm down, your Holiness... You shouldn't get all worked up... Don't forget, you're going to have to address all those journalists, and there's nothing they'd like better...

SECOND NUN: ...than to see you throwing a wobbly... You know what? I think you're a bit of an old reactionary.

POPE: Reactionary? Me? The cheek of it! I tell you, Sister, I'm a lot more progressive than you think. Anyway, you heard it for yourself – here I am, the head of the Church, and I have high-up members of the clergy standing up and preaching against me. But what do I do? I don't go off and sentence them to death, as Ayatollah Khomeini would do... Mind you, would that I had the chance! Ha, ha!

SECOND NUN: I'd like to hear you say *that* in front of the journalists.

POPE: They'd never get the joke! [*To the PRIEST*.] Carry on.

[*The MUSICIANS strike up again.*]

PRIEST: The man from the *Frankfurter Allgemeine* wants to know your feelings about the statement made by Deacon Keller from Holland, who has declared himself opposed to your statement in which...

POPE: Me, statement, what statement? Give it here, let me read it for myself. [*He takes some papers from the PRIEST.*]

PROFESSOR: You should try and read them with detachment, your Holiness.

POPE: Of course... How's this for detachment...?! [*He holds the papers at arm's length, and chuckles.*] Vatican humour! Relax, I can control myself. Here, look, he says: "I recall that in the nineteenth century, Pope Pius IX..." Who's talking here? Ah, it's still Keller... "In the nineteenth century Pope Pius IX used to issue condemnations of doctors who vaccinated people suffering from cholera. [*The music stops.*] Vaccination, he declared, was an act contrary to nature." [*To the FIRST CARDINAL.*] Is it true, what he says?

FIRST CARDINAL: Unfortunately, yes, your Holiness. Word for word.

POPE: Oh dear... Pius IX... may the Lord rest his soul... Well, let's carry on. [*He continues reading, and the music strikes up again.*] "Then, when there was an epidemic and it was beginning to kill large numbers of people, the Pontiff was obliged to change his tune, and declared that: 'Vaccination is not a question of dogma!' And later on, when a number of dying bishops were actually saved by vaccination, he said: 'Well, of course, Pasteur, the discoverer of the vaccine, was inspired by Providence in his discovery, even if he was a notorious atheist.'" But this is too much, this is scandalous...!

[*The music stops again.*]

PROFESSOR: Your Holiness, I thought you said you were able to control yourself? Anyway, I have to admit, I've read about Pius IX's statements too... What Keller says is historically undeniable... So...

POPE: So what? What's Keller getting at, and this jumped-up journalist too...? I suppose they're trying to make a parallel between me and Pius IX. Seeing that I preach that the use of contraceptives is contrary to nature, I suppose they're saying that I'm reactionary and obscurantist, just like Pius IX... And maybe, next, they're expecting me to come out with a statement that: [*The music starts again.*] "Contraception is not a question of dogma! And Condom, the inventor of the first rubber... condom... was obviously inspired by the Holy Ghost!" [*As he says this, he flings his arms open and leans forward. All of a sudden he has a muscular seizure, and is left standing with his arms and legs apart. The music breaks off.*] Ouch...! [*He moves his arms, in an attempt to straighten himself up, but cannot.*] Ouuuch!

PROFESSOR: [*Worried; running over to the POPE.*] What's happened, your Holiness?

POPE: I seem to have had some kind of a seizure... Didn't you see? Just as I stretched out my arms... Crack! I felt a sort of crack right across my kidneys... across between my shoulder blades too... I'm stuck. I can't move...

FIRST CARDINAL: Oh Lord, this is all we need!

[*Everybody comes over to the POPE, including the MUSICIANS, to stop him falling over.*]

PROFESSOR: Don't try to move! [*He hands the POPE a spear and also the pole on which the sculpted Pope's head is placed.*] Lean on these, your Holiness.

POPE: Oh thank you... Oof, that feels better already...

PROFESSOR: [*To the FIRST NUN.*] Sister, help him out of his clothes.

[*As the FIRST NUN lays her hands on the POPE's shoulders, he lets out a yell.*]

POPE: Ouch, no! Don't touch me!

PROFESSOR: What do you mean, "Don't touch me"? You're not shy of nuns, are you?

POPE: No, it's just that when she touched my skin it felt like I was being sandpapered with a Black and Decker... Ouch...!

PROFESSOR: Let me feel for a moment...

[*He reaches out his hands to touch the POPE's back.*]

POPE: Go easy, for goodness sake... [*The PROFESSOR touches him.*] Ouch! Ouuuch!

[*The PROFESSOR and the FIRST NUN remove the POPE's upper garment, leaving him in a shirt and baggy trousers.*]

PROFESSOR: I would say the symptoms are obvious... A classic case of hyperaesthesia.

POPE: Classic...? What's hyperaesthesia? Is it serious? How do I end up getting it?

PROFESSOR: Well, at the origins, I would say that it was probably a sciatic neuralgia of the lumbar region, otherwise known as the "witch's stroke".

[*Aided by the SECOND NUN he pulls out of his doctor's bag the wherewithals for measuring the POPE's blood pressure.*]

POPE: Well now that's a real laugh... The Pope, noted scourge of the feminists, in other words today's witches, gets struck down by the classic witch's stroke!

SECOND NUN: [*She laughs.*] I'm glad to see you've still got a sense of humour, your Holiness!

POPE: Ha, ha...! The only trouble is, every time I laugh, it gives me a terrible pain, right here in the back.

PROFESSOR: That's easily explained. When you laugh, the movement involved means that the sciatic nerve gets rubbed between your vertebrae, all adding up to a classic slipped disc, with sciatic complications.

POPE: Classic, eh? Well, I'm glad we're still dealing with the classics!

PROFESSOR: What's more, I would say that what we have here is almost certainly an anchylosant spondylitis, involving the upper vertebrae, the atlantis and the epistrophe.

POPE: Anchylosant spondylitis... atlantis and epistrophe... What is this, Virgil's Aeneid?!

PROFESSOR: And by extension this leads to what we doctors call the "crucifixion stroke".

POPE: Also classic, I presume...! So in addition to the witch's stroke, I've got crucifixion stroke too?

PROFESSOR: Exactly.

POPE: Well, that's handy, I suppose I am a Pope, and the cross is my symbol after all.

FIRST CARDINAL: If you'll excuse me, I suppose I'll have to go and send the journalists away again... Today just isn't my day!

[*He exits.*]

POPE: Did you see that? He doesn't even *care* about my crucifixion stroke... All he's interested in is newspapers...! Newspapers and journalists, journalists and newspapers...! Anyway, what about this "hyperaesthesia", which, as I recall, was also classic.

PROFESSOR: Well, I was just coming to that, your Holiness; it's all part of what we doctors know as the pathological hunchback syndrome.

POPE: Hunchback...? All of a sudden I'm a hunchback...? Things aren't going too well for me today. Perhaps I ought to get someone's blessing, just in case.

PROFESSOR: Don't get too upset. I know this is rather a lot to be coping with...

SECOND NUN: That's right.. All at one go, eh?

PROFESSOR: In these cases you always find symptoms of paraesthesia – you could call it referred pain – caused by a malfunctioning of the sympathetic ganglia.

POPE: Excuse me Professor... I don't follow... What exactly is malfunctioning here?

PROFESSOR: The sympathetic ganglia. You see, in the area around the plexus... we have a network of ganglia that act as a kind of coordinating centre... a sort of telephone exchange, if you like... one on either side. These receive and interpret commands from the brain... and then pass them to other parts of the body. You follow me?

POPE: I suppose so. It must be a bit like the internal workings of the Holy See, which, by the way, is also made up of two chambers.

PROFESSOR: Exactly, well done... But now, your Holiness, imagine that all of a sudden the nerve centre starts receiving signals which are unclear and confused, because of a breakdown in the sciatic system... What happens?

POPE: The Holy See goes haywire.

PROFESSOR: Exactly. The lines start to overheat, your nerves become over-sensitised, and they create this burning sensation, so that all it needs is for someone even just to touch your skin and you end up howling like a coyote! Clear?

POPE: So... to sum up: I, personally, Holy Father to the whole of Christianity, all eight hundred million of them, in fact more like a billion, find myself with my ganglia malfunctioning... my brain on the blink... a hump on my back which derives from my sympathetic doo-da... a classic witch's stroke... a common-or-garden crucifixion stroke... nerve signals blacking out all round... a slipped disc... the Holy See gone haywire, and I can't even laugh because if I do my vertebrae go scritch-scritch... and I howl like a coyote... and at that moment Gruber Kutter arrives, the Bishop of Cologne whom I put out to pasture with the goats, and he falls about laughing.

[*The POPE gets agitated, and as he leans forward he loses his balance and tumbles forward on the spear and the pole on which he was leaning. The music breaks off.*]

PROFESSOR: Look out!

SECOND NUN: Don't just stand there, give him a hand!

FIRST CARDINAL: Hold him up!

POPE: Help! It's the curse of Gruber Kutter!

[*The PROFESSOR and the BYSTANDERS rush forward to lift the POPE up.*]

PROFESSOR: Have you hurt yourself, your Holiness?

POPE: No, only a big bash on the nose! I'm sure I've broken a couple of ribs as well, but apart from that I'm fine.

FIRST CARDINAL: Relax, your Holiness! Sit down.

POPE: Is there a chair there?

FIRST CARDINAL: Yes, yes... sit down... Relax, your Holiness...

POPE: [*He sits down.*] I suppose that's right... I should relax! I'm wondering why exactly the Lord has decided to lay me low like this...

FIRST CARDINAL: The Lord is putting you to the test, as a sign of his love for you!

POPE: Couldn't he love some of you a little bit as well, though?

PROFESSOR: Well, cheer up your Holiness. [*To the SECOND NUN.*] Flectadol! [*To the POPE.*] Maybe in a minute or two your suffering will be at an end... Always assuming that you're willing to collaborate.

[*The SECOND NUN prepares the hypodermic, goes over to the POPE, and prepares to give the injection.*]

POPE: What made you think that I wouldn't be willing...? More to the point, how are you planning to get me out of this wretched situation? [*Referring to the injection.*] What's that?

PROFESSOR: A pain killer.

POPE: Classic?

PROFESSOR: Common-or-garden.

POPE: Ouch! For a pain killer, it's very... painful! And is this going to cure me of everything?

PROFESSOR: No, unfortunately not. Your Holiness, to be perfectly honest, in the area of neurosympathology and sciatic disorders, modern Western medicine is basically at point zero.

POPE: Oh good, that's really cheered me up.

PROFESSOR: When it comes to this kind of illness, any witch doctor in Africa would have a set of diagnostic techniques and cures far more effective than anything that we have at our disposal.

POPE: Ah, here we go again with your mania for exotic cures and native medicines!

PROFESSOR: Your Holiness, I assure you that in Africa I personally have been present at cases of blockage similar to yours... and the Sister here can testify to that.

POPE: Ah, was she down there too?

SECOND NUN: Yes, I was...

POPE: And how did they cure them?

SECOND NUN: The commonest method consisted of smearing the patient's back with honey, and then applying an entire nest of rather angry red ants, which had previously been agitated by giving them a good smoke-up with Afghan hashish, and then, hopla, the patient would leap up and go running off into the savannah singing Hallelujah! Hallelujah!

POPE: Professor, if you so much as try that on me, I'll have you thrown out of every medical order on the

planet... covered with ants in your turn, and with a
bonfire stuck... I won't say where! And then we'll see
you running off into the savannah... but I'll be the one
who'll be singing the Hallelujahs...

PROFESSOR: All right, your Holiness, if you put it like
that, I surrender.

POPE: No need to get all touchy... Can't a Pope have a
joke every once in a while? Even though I don't know
how I manage it. At this precise point I feel so
completely wretched that if you were to put me in the
hands of a Bantu witch doctor... in fact, do me a
favour, phone and see if you can get me one, would
you? I've heard such a lot of good things about that De
Michelis... Couldn't you get him along?

SECOND NUN: No, there's no need to start phoning
around, your Holiness. You'll just have to imagine that
I'm a Bantu witch doctor... If you'd be willing to trust
me, I'd like to try a very particular kind of cure.

POPE: At this point I'm game for anything, so go ahead.

SECOND NUN: All right. Now, first of all we have to
find a way of raising your Holiness to about this height
[*She raises a hand to eye level.*] and in such a way that you
can completely relax your back muscles.

[*The POPE is helped to lean forward.*]

FIRST CARDINAL: And how do you propose doing
that? If we're starting lifting games, I'd better go and
get a couple of Swiss Guards.

[*He exits, and returns immediately, followed by two
SWISS GUARDS.*]

SECOND NUN: Tell you what – why don't we lower that
chandelier. Then we could use the ropes.

PRIEST: Good idea.

POPE: What does this "treatment" involve?

[*The chandelier is lowered.*]

SECOND NUN: Unhook the chandelier... [*Everyone helps. The ropes which hold up the chandelier are converted into a sort of harness for the POPE.*] Shift that table... Make a loop under the Holy Father's armpits, and another one under his stomach... and one supporting his legs... There, that looks fine. Now raise him up.

[*The two SWISS GUARDS haul on the ropes, and the POPE is hoisted into position.*]

POPE: Couldn't I have a couple of candles too? I'd make a good baroque chandelier.

[*The PROFESSOR, aided by the SISTER, pushes a table and a stool across to where the POPE is suspended in mid-air.*]

PROFESSOR: [*To the SECOND NUN.*] Climb up on this table, you'll be able to reach his Holiness more easily.

SECOND NUN: Good thinking... Give me a hand. [*To the FIRST NUN.*] Sister, would you get me a basin of boiling water?

[*The FIRST NUN exits.*]

POPE: Boiling water? What do you want with boiling water?

SECOND NUN: Don't worry, your Holiness, I'm not about to pour it over you. [*To the FIRST CARDINAL.*] Your Eminence, would you get some incense and four candles and set them up round here.

POPE: Candles?! What is this – the funeral, already?

[*The MUSICIANS exit, and re-enter with large candle-holders, which are placed on either side of the POPE. They are followed by a SWISS GUARD carrying incense, and by a PRIEST carrying a large silver basin, which is placed on the ground beneath the POPE. As each character walks in front of the POPE, they genuflect. The POPE responds*] *with strangely contorted movements of his head and upper torso.*]

POPE: [*At the end of the procession.*] Wonderful. When do the Three Wise Men arrive?

SECOND NUN: Professor, in my handbag you'll find a small tobacco pouch with some crystals in it. As the water comes to the boil, throw a dozen of them in. [*She leans across the POPE's back.*] Your Holiness, please, relax...

POPE: I can't... I'm sorry... I'm just all tensed up...

[*The FIRST NUN re-enters.*]

FIRST NUN: Here's the boiling water...

SECOND NUN: Give it to the Professor.

[*The PROFESSOR pours the water into the basin and adds the crystals. This produces a large number of soap bubbles which float up underneath the POPE. The MUSICIANS and the SWISS GUARDS arrange themselves around the POPE as he hangs suspended.*]

Now, I want you to imagine that you are somewhere completely different... imagine you're in the sea somewhere... Swimming... I want big movements of your arms... and I want to hear you singing... [*To the SWISS GUARDS.*] And you... Set this contraption swinging a bit, and light the candles too.

[*The POPE is swung slowly to and fro in the harness; the SECOND NUN spreads her hands over him.*]

POPE: Sing, you say? Well, I'll give it a try. [*He begins intoning a Gregorian chant, which is immediately taken up by the STRING QUARTET.*] Aleus Domine Fulgitur...

SECOND NUN: What on earth kind of song do you call that?

POPE: It's Gregorian...

SECOND NUN: Who ever heard of anybody swimming and singing in Gregorian?

POPE: Lefebvre does.

SECOND NUN: Can't we have something a bit more lively!

POPE: Lively? There's no such thing as lively Gregorian chant!

SECOND NUN: Don't you know any proper songs? What about when you were a boy? You *were* a boy once, weren't you?

POPE: Yes, but not for long.

SECOND NUN: You must remember some little song from your childhood?

POPE: Yes, now I think of it, there was one. It went something like this:

[*He sings.*]

Strado je hobje alonnideja
Strado-je-nubie alfonida

SECOND NUN: That's brilliant... Carry on.

[*The STRING QUARTET provides a musical backing.*]

POPE: [*He sings in Slavic.*]

Acuni bonnja inanolijae
A la-stoni-nijamihiae acooinaat!

SECOND NUN: Carry on with the singing... In a minute or two you'll feel a sensation of heat coming over you. Perfect! [*To the PROFESSOR and FIRST CARDINAL.*] Come on, you sing too!

FIRST CARDINAL: I can't sing in Slavic!

SECOND NUN: Well mime, then... Where there's a will there's a way.

[*Everybody sings along with the POPE.*]

ALL:

Strado je hobje alonnideja
Strado-je-nubie alfonida
Acuni bonnja inanolijae

[*All of a sudden, the SECOND CARDINAL enters (the priest in charge of Vatican security). He is holding a photograph, and is accompanied by two SWISS GUARDS.*]

SECOND CARDINAL: Excuse my interrupting, your Holiness, but we have a serious problem here... We have incontrovertible evidence...

[*He stops in his tracks and stares in amazement at the scene of the suspended POPE swinging to and fro.*]

POPE: I was starting to feel better just now... Now all of a sudden I feel like someone's shot me full of quick-setting cement.

SECOND CARDINAL: [*He goes over to the SECOND NUN and climbs up onto the stool next to her in order to compare her face with the face in the photograph.*] Yes, it's her. Absolutely no doubt at all!

[*He gestures to the SWISS GUARDS, who come over to arrest her.*]

POPE: [*Stopping them.*] What on earth has got into you? Since when have people had the right to come wandering round my chambers, not to mention climbing up on my furniture, without so much as a "by your leave"...?

FIRST CARDINAL: And right in the middle of a Slavic song, too!

SECOND CARDINAL: But we have a serious security problem here!

SECOND NUN: I think I should warn you, if we don't re-start the massage at once, we'll be right back where we started and the Pope's going to seize up again.

PROFESSOR: [*He climbs up on a stool next to the SECOND CARDINAL.*] Speaking as the doctor responsible for His Holiness's health, your Eminence, I'm afraid I'm going to have to ask you to leave!

SECOND CARDINAL: I'm sorry, but as head of Vatican security, Professor, I must insist that I stay and carry out my duty, and I must inform you about the real origins and profession of this... woman...

POPE: That's enough of that! What is this, a rank and file ecclesiastical take-over?!

FIRST CARDINAL: We already know; the Sister works in a community centre rehabilitating drug addicts... she's a qualified healer...

SECOND CARDINAL: A qualified healer, maybe. But she has absolutely no licence or permit to practise. She's running an illegal operation in other words. [*To the GUARDS.*] Get those nun's clothes off her and take her away, she's a sham...

POPE: Get her clothes off? You're going to start undressing a nun? Here? In my apartments? What is this? The Crazy Horse Saloon?

PROFESSOR: I'm afraid you've gone a bit too far, your Eminence! Interrupting a crucial moment of the andro-therapeutic process... Do you want the Holy Father to be the victim of an irreversible arthritic paroxysm?

SECOND CARDINAL: What if I were to tell you that this so-called "Sister" from Burundi was not in fact a missionary... that this woman...

POPE: So why should I worry whether she's a missionary nun in Burundi or a convent nun in Monte Cenisio?

Ouuuch...! I'm seizing up again! Get out...! Get out...! You, and your Switzers!

SECOND CARDINAL: Your Holiness, the only reason I'm here is to save your life.

POPE: What do you mean, save my life? I see no danger? People love me... The political situation is under control...

SECOND CARDINAL: Exactly. The same words that President Ceaucescu said five minutes before they shot him.

[*Exit the SECOND CARDINAL, followed by the SWISS GUARDS.*]

POPE: The cheek of the man! Now how on earth am I going to relax again...

SECOND NUN: You'd best start singing again.

POPE: Easier said than done... I've lost the motivation.

SECOND NUN: [*With her hands still laid on the POPE.*] I'll see if I can give you a hand, then. I know a little song with just the same tune as yours. They used to sing it in the village where I lived, when I was a girl.

POPE: Really?

SECOND NUN: Yes, of course. You listen and tell me if it isn't the same. [*She sings.*]

Oh fresh rose, the weather is so gentle
Come down, come down, don't make me wait for you.
Undress yourself, take off all your petals,
And come and sink
Into this clear, warm water.
You are a mermaid among the waves.
With your eyes you take me to the bottom of the sea.
You take me to the bottom of the sea.
You take me to the bottom of the sea.

POPE: Naughty, naughty...! My song didn't have rude bits in it... Two lovers in the water, getting undressed... Sinking into warm water and getting up to hanky-panky... Without any clothes on, too.

SECOND NUN: What do you mean, two lovers? They're married!

POPE: No, I'm sorry... People who go getting undressed in warm water... and embracing each other with no clothes on aren't married! And if they are married, they're certainly not married to each other.

SECOND NUN: Before you start... pontif-icating... could I draw your attention to the fact that you just started moving your arms about as if there was nothing wrong with you?!

POPE: Amazing! I didn't even notice. It must have been the singing that did it.

SECOND NUN: Come on... Relax, move about a bit more... Don't worry...

POPE: Alright, I'll try. Let me down... I want to try walking a bit...

PROFESSOR: Right. Help him down.

[*Everyone helps the POPE to come down.*]

POPE: [*When he reaches ground level, he begins to move, swivelling his legs and his body in a disjointed fashion.*] Yes, I can do it! Look how well I move! Strutting like a peacock!

FIRST CARDINAL: What an amazing recovery! Fling open the windows, the Pope is cured!

SECOND NUN: Slow down, don't get carried away... The first time round the effect doesn't last for very long.

[*As FIRST NUN flings open the windows, the SECOND CARDINAL enters, followed by two SWISS GUARDS.*]

SECOND CARDINAL: I'm sorry to interrupt again, your Holiness... this really is extremely urgent... I insist that you let me explain.

POPE: In a minute, if you don't mind. First I want to thank this Sister.

[*The STRING QUARTET begins playing again, quietly.*]

POPE: Now, I think the time has come... Would you all sit down and listen... [*The music breaks off.*] The Cardinal here has been trying to tell me that this Sister...

SECOND NUN: Is not a nun at all...

POPE: What? How do you mean?

SECOND NUN: Like he says. I'm not a nun...

POPE: You are a missionary, though?

SECOND NUN: I'm afraid not.

POPE: And you don't even come from Burundi?

SECOND NUN: Yes, I do come from Burundi. And how...

POPE: Well, at least there was a bit of truth in it. Oh dear oh dear... I guessed it as soon as you came in... There was something in the way you moved... And then when I got hit by my "witch's stroke"... I had my mind on too many other things. So who *are* you, then?

SECOND NUN: A witch. Like he said.

POPE: What...?! I do hope you're joking.

PROFESSOR: Of course she is, your Holiness. My assistant has a rather bizarre sense of humour...

SECOND NUN: Why don't we just call it a day, Professor, and stop pretending. [*To the POPE.*] Yes, I'm exactly that... a witch. My life story is so amazing that they've been begging me to make a 139-episode TV series out of it.

POPE: I hope we're not going to get the full version now... I'm due to leave for Moscow on Thursday.

SECOND NUN: I could give you a quick run-down.

POPE: All right. Let's have the potted version.

SECOND NUN: Well, I was born in Africa, to white parents, who went and died in a hunting accident. I was looked after by a Bantu witch doctor, who reared me like a mother. At the age of nine I was walking on burning coals; at the age of ten I was walking on water... not least, to cool my feet, because of the fire. At the age of twelve, a herd of wild elephants was about to trample my village. I stood in front of them, raised my arms, and let out a terrifying yell! The elephants were stopped in their tracks... and two rhinoceroses came and lay down at my feet and went: "Ee-eee-eee", which is rhinoceroses' way of communicating with humans... and they said: "Here we are, prostrate at your feet... Do with us what you will... We are willing to do anything... Even change our names... if you'll only let us join the Socialist International, like the Italian Communist Party." End of the first episode. The second episode...

POPE: [*Interrupting her.*] No, no, spare us...

SECOND NUN: But it's the bit where I meet Tarzan! He was running the World Wildlife Fund at the time!

POPE: Very funny! [*To the PROFESSOR.*] Leaving aside this woman's unorthodox qualifications, what on earth put it into your head to bring her here dressed as a nun?

PROFESSOR: First of all, I had to find some way of getting her into the Vatican and smuggling her past your Swiss Guards. And then, to be honest, would you have accepted her otherwise?

POPE: Well, I don't know, really... I suppose she seems pretty reliable... I don't see a problem...

SECOND CARDINAL: Well there *is* a problem, your Holiness, and how... as I was trying to tell you a short while ago... You ask this fraudster to spell out her real profession, and you will find that what we have here is a drug-trafficker, who also happens to specialise in illegal abortions.

SECOND NUN: Whoops! That's blown it!

POPE: You do abortions! An abortionist?!

PROFESSOR: Let's keep it in proportion... She works in a therapeutic community, where completely legal doctors carry out minor operations.

POPE: And abortions! Do you realise the position you've put me in? I'm talking to you, Professor, and [*To the FIRST CARDINAL.*] you! Personal secretary, indeed! Don't you dare let a word of this get out to the Press!

SECOND NUN: [*Picking up her bags.*] Isn't life amazing... Up until a few minutes ago I was this extraordinary, marvellous woman... and now I'm the nun who never was!

POPE: You have dreamed up this diabolical situation... an insult to my person, and to everything I represent. When I think that you allowed this wretched woman to put her hands on me, the same murderous hands that have killed innocent babies before they could see the light of day.

SECOND NUN: Excuse me, your Holiness, but let's get one thing straight. Personally speaking, I am not in favour of abortions either... but if it's a choice between that and the horrors of the alternative, with desperate women dying of back-street abortions every day, I think I know which side I come down on. It's only with great reluctance and pain that I take that path, believe me.

POPE: You can't fool me with fancy words!

SECOND NUN: You protest about my hands, but it never worried you to shake certain other hands. The truly bloodstained hands of the likes of President Pinochet and President Marcos, and that other dictatorial thug in El Salvador.

POPE: [*To the SECOND CARDINAL.*] Cardinal!

SECOND CARDINAL: Your Holiness?

POPE: I don't want to hear another word out of that woman! Get her out! Out of my sight!

SECOND CARDINAL: [*To the SWISS GUARDS.*] Do as he says.

[*The SWISS GUARDS frog-march the SECOND NUN to the exit.*]

POPE: Take those nun's clothes off her, and hand her over to the police of the country she belongs to. No, more to the point, just see her to the door. Get her out, I said!

SECOND NUN: That's fine, your Holiness. Enjoy your seizure!

[*The SWISS GUARDS march her off.*]

POPE: Get out!

[*He gestures as if to shoo her off, and his arms lock in the same outstretched position as previously.*]

FIRST CARDINAL: There! She's done it! She's done it! She's given him another seizure!

PROFESSOR: So what do we do now?

[*The SECOND NUN comes running back on stage.*]

SECOND NUN: Maybe I can be of assistance.

GENERAL CHORUS: Get her off!

[*The SECOND NUN raises her arms and lets out a screech. Everyone on stage is convulsed, as if by an electric shock, and they end up with their arms in the same outstretched position as the POPE. The SECOND NUN exits.*]

[*Musical interlude. Blackout.*]

ACT TWO

SCENE 1

[*We find ourselves in a warehouse or a large and more or less dilapidated room. The windows are in a state of disrepair, and there is a skylight in the ceiling. There is glass missing from some of the windows. The room is bare. In the centre stands a long table. On-stage we see a group of YOUNG MEN AND WOMEN. They look pale and undernourished. It is clear that they are drug addicts. They are at work on weaving looms.*

The HEALER, whom we saw previously in the guise of the SECOND NUN, is now dressed simply in a doctor's jacket and a pair of trousers. She is busy massaging a YOUTH who is stretched out on the table. From backstage, enter the PROFESSOR. The YOUTHS run up to him, shouting excitedly in unison and trying to search him.]

PROFESSOR: Do you mind?!

FIRST BOY: He's arrived! It's him!

FIRST GIRL: Have you got the stuff?

THIRD BOY: Are you the courier?

PROFESSOR: Hey, calm down, get your hands off!

HEALER: Stop that! Leave him alone! He's got nothing to do with it, it can't be him... He's a Professor.

FIRST BOY: So? Why couldn't it be a Professor who brings us the stuff?

HEALER: Leave him alone, I said!

[*They all return to what they were doing.*]

PROFESSOR: What on earth was that all about...? What were they all after?

HEALER: Nothing, nothing... Just a misunderstanding, don't worry about it, Professor...

PROFESSOR: Alright. Anyway, I sent you some medical supplies and things. Did you receive them?

HEALER: Yes. Thank you... [*She finishes massaging the BOY and sends him packing.*] Whose turn is it now?

ASSISTANT: [*To one of the GIRLS.*] Come on, you're next..

PROFESSOR: Hey, now this is a lovely welcome! You're not angry with me too, are you?

HEALER: Not at all... It's just that I'm under a lot of pressure... I have problems... Anyway, spit it out — what do you want this time?

PROFESSOR: Well, I only dropped in to say hello, really... To find out how you're getting on.

HEALER: Well, that's really lovely, Professor. "Hello. What a lovely day. How nice to see you!" And now, the door's over there. Give my regards to the family.

[*She pushes him towards the door.*]

PROFESSOR: You can't throw me out just like that... We worked together once... we were friends...

HEALER: Spare me the "old pals" act. I presume you've come here for a reason. I hope you're not trying to convince me to pay another visit to... the fellow with the funny hat...?

PROFESSOR: No, not at all! I don't think we need go to the Vatican again.

HEALER: Just as well.

PROFESSOR: He's decided he's coming here, instead.

HEALER: Who?

PROFESSOR: The fellow with the funny hat. In person.

HEALER: Here? To me? Are you crazy?

PROFESSOR: Almost!... Seeing that the mountain won't go to Mohammed...

HEALER: So I'm a mountain, now? I'm warning you, if he's coming looking for political asylum, I'll hand him straight over to the Americans. Moody old bastard, isn't he! One minute he's falling at my feet, just because he's feeling a bit peeky, and the next minute he's calling me a murderer.

PROFESSOR: The poor chap is at his wits' end. He's totally seized up. We've tried everything... electric shocks... acupuncture... poking around in his sympathetic ganglia... Nothing! At a certain point he was so desperate that he started asking for you again.

HEALER: Spare me the sob stories, Professor, because I'll start to cry. So how will His Nibs be arriving? Unobtrusively in his white Popemobile, I suppose?

PROFESSOR: No, not at all... He's coming totally incognito... dressed in ordinary clothes. Don't say no... I'm relying on you...

HEALER: Well, I suppose, when all's said and done, the Pope's a Christian too, eh? Alright, where is he? I bet he's waiting at the door.

PROFESSOR: You guessed it! I brought him with me... Allow me...

[*He gestures with his hand, and the POPE enters from backstage. He is wearing inconspicuous dark clothes, with a corduroy jacket and a collarless shirt. He has his arms up in the air, and in an effort to disguise this unusual position he carries a basket on his head, containing fruit and vegetables.*]

POPE: Good morning.

HEALER: Oh my goodness, look at the state of him...!

[*The BOYS and GIRLS get excited again and dive on him.*]

FIRST BOY: Here he is!

THIRD BOY: In the basket, the stuff must be in the basket!

SECOND BOY: This time it really is him.

POPE: Hey, hold on... Get off... What's got into you?

FIRST GIRL: Where is it, where have you hidden it?

[*One of the BOYS grabs the POPE's basket, leaving him with his arms up in the air.*]

SECOND GIRL: [*Searching through the basket.*] I bet they've hidden it among the vegetables.

POPE: What's got into them?

HEALER: Leave him alone. He's nothing to do with it! He's not the courier... That's enough, now!

POPE: What are they looking for, though?

PROFESSOR: They did the same to me – came leaping all over me...

HEALER: Goodness, you really are in a state. [*She accompanies him to a chair.*] Here, sit down.

SECOND GIRL: What's he doing with his arms up in the air? I bet he's some sort of Hindu holy man.

FIRST BOY: But if he's not the courier either, then who is? The stuff's usually been here by now.

HEALER: How should I know... Just hang on a bit, eh?

SECOND GIRL: Hey, no! I can't stand it any more, I'm feeling bad.

HEALER: And who cares if you feel bad...? Look at this poor gentleman... He's certainly in a worse state than you, and he's not complaining, is he?

SECOND GIRL: I'm not a Holy Man like him, though.

PROFESSOR: What are they waiting for?

HEALER: A free delivery of something rather special.

PROFESSOR: And who's supposed to be bringing it?

HEALER: Nobody knows.

POPE: It wouldn't happen to be the packet I've got in my pocket, would it?

HEALER: You've got a packet in your pocket?

POPE: Yes. A transparent packet. Somebody slipped it into my jacket outside... while I was waiting to come in.

FIRST BOY: Hey, the Hindu's got the packet!

THIRD BOY: Where is it? Which pocket?

[*The YOUTHS dive on him and knock him to the floor.*]

FIRST GIRL: Come on, Hindu! Let's have it.

HEALER: [*She helps the POPE to get up.*] Stop that, or I'll put the lot of you out the door! [*She sits him back on his chair.*] God help anyone who lays so much as a hand on him!

SECOND GIRL: So who is he, then? God Almighty?

HEALER: Let's say he's the next best thing.

FIRST BOY: It looks like he's stuck in that position!

HEALER: If you don't mind, your Holi... I mean, may I...?

POPE: There, right there... in the inside pocket...

HEALER: [*She pulls a packet out of the pocket of the POPE's jacket.*] Yes. That's the one we're waiting for.

CHORUS: Hey!

POPE: The fellow outside told me: "Give it to Elisa." Who's Elisa?

HEALER: I'm Elisa.

POPE: You're Elisa? Pleased to meet you...

HEALER: [*To the YOUTH.*] And now, calm down, all of you, and line up, and I'll do your shots. [*To the POPE.*] You'll have to excuse you, a moment. I'll just get them sorted out, and I'll be with you right away.

POPE: So you're not angry with me any more?

HEALER: I don't have the time to nurse old grudges... You need time on your hands for that sort of thing.

POPE: But when I threw you out the other day, you were absolutely furious...

HEALER: True... I get that way every once in a while... Anyway, make yourself at home. [*To her ASSISTANT.*] Hey, get a move on with those needles... I'm almost ready [*To a BOY who is trying to take a syringe.*] Mitts off...! Professor, give me a hand.

[*One of the GIRLS brings over to the HEALER a hospital trolley loaded with bottles, test-tubes, small bowls, various instruments and a small spirit lamp. The HEALER measures out a dose, breaks open an ampoule and mixes the mixture into a container. She takes a syringe and prepares the first injection.*]

PROFESSOR: Excuse me, am I mistaken, or are you just about to...

HEALER: No, you're not mistaken. [*To the YOUTHS.*] Who's first? [*They all rush forward, noisily.*] Stop! Get in a queue.

[*She sits one of the BOYS down.*]

PROFESSOR: But what *is* that you're injecting?

HEALER: Heroin.

PROFESSOR AND POPE: What?!

POPE: Heroin? So that transparent packet that I was carrying was...

HEALER: That's right. Heroin. One hundred per cent Grade A heroin.

POPE: You mean I've been carrying drugs?! Imagine what would have happened if I'd been stopped by a policeman...

HEALER: We would have had the finest scandal of the century.

POPE: And you think it's funny...! I can't handle this any more... My arms are getting tired.

HEALER: Hang onto that iron crossbar over there, in the alcove... It could have been made for you... Anyway, I don't inject the stuff full-strength... It'd blow their minds... I make up a mixture. I've added Arsenofix as a vein-dilator, together with some fluidifying Merenal, and various other secret specialities of the house.

POPE: But what do you mean...? You're handing out drug injections in a place like this?

HEALER: Yes, you're right, the place is a bit squalid; I suppose it would be better if it had a bit more atmosphere... comfortable sofas... hubbly-bubblies... soft music...

[*Aided by her ASSISTANT she sets about the business of giving injections to all the drug addicts.*]

POPE: Don't go making jokes about it... It's insane, what you're doing.

HEALER: Insane situations require insane solutions. I can't see any other way round it, for the moment.

POPE: No other way? What about you, Professor? Have you nothing to say?

SECOND GIRL: Oh dear, the Hindu's kicking up a fuss!

PROFESSOR: Well, I am astonished and perplexed.

POPE: What do you mean – this woman's engaged in wholesale drug trafficking, and all you can say is that you're astonished and perplexed?!

HEALER: Gently! Who's trafficking? What happens here is that we supply the drugs at a controlled price. Dealers out on the street would charge you 50,000 lire for a dose, but we sell a dose for 1,800... And that includes injection, with a clean needle, and under medical control... [*She points to her ASSISTANT.*] She's a doctor... A drug addict, but a doctor nevertheless.

SECOND GIRL: And if you haven't got the money, you can even get it on tick.

POPE: But don't you realise that you are promoting moral corruption, and vice, and criminality...!

HEALER: Excuse me, but you're talking like Mary Whitehouse. If anything, it's quite the opposite! Take this boy, for example. [*She points to one of the BOYS.*] Out on the street, if he wants to get the money for his daily shot, he has to deal at least ten doses to other young people like himself, or find new ones that he can persuade onto the habit... [*To the FIRST GIRL.*] Tell this gentleman how you get to afford your drugs.

FIRST GIRL: I'm on the game...

HEALER: That's no way to put it...! You're in the business of offering remunerated affection... Her over there, on the other hand, she's in the business of thieving. And that one over there's into thieving too, but unfortunately he's not very good, so he spends most of his time *doing* time. There's others too. You'll see them later... when the night shift comes. Good kids, all of them. All in and out of prison most of the time.

POPE: So you run a shift-system, eh?

FIRST BOY: That's right, Holy Man... Spot on!
Sometimes we do upwards of fifty sittings a day.

POPE: Hey, no, look! I'm sorry, but I can't stay in a place
like this...! I guess I'll just have to learn to live with my
seizure...

[*He heads for the exit.*]

HEALER: Ah, so you're disgusted... I quite understand...
Go ahead, leave! But what do you think – that I pump
this filthy poison into these kids because I'm some kind
of depraved pervert? No, it horrifies me... Maybe even
more than you. Every time... every time I do it, I feel
sick in my stomach. It makes me want to throw up.

POPE: Nobody's forcing you to do it, though.. So why do it?

HEALER: It's the idea that somehow, in some little way, I
might be doing somebody some good. If nothing else,
ever since we opened this place and started making the
drugs available at reduced prices, it seems like we've
already started to have an effect. For example, take
these young men and women. We can give them more
choice in life than just prostitution, Aids, a life of crime
and prison. They're here, and that gives me a chance
of talking to them... and reasoning with them... and
maybe even getting them to do something useful with
their lives.

POPE: Stupendous! First you shoot them full of cheap
drugs, and then you "reason" with them? This is
heaven on earth...! In fact, even better than Heaven,
because in the Garden of Eden the apples were
forbidden, and here they get their shots for free.

HEALER: Please, don't start making fun of me. These
kids are trying to stay alive and healthy until such time
as they manage to kick the drugs... Because people
don't necessarily die of heroin, but when you get Aids,
you die, and that's that.

POPE: But doesn't it occur to you that these poor creatures only come here and listen to you because you're handing out drugs left right and centre?

GIRL: Hey, it sounds like our Guru isn't too keen on us, eh?

PROFESSOR: Exactly, they see no further than their next fix. You can't *reason* with them...

POPE: But on the other hand I suppose we should have compassion on them... they are our children, after all, and they have plunged into the abyss of a terrible alienation...

PROFESSOR: And the business of pulling them back is going to be long and hard.

HEALER: So in the meantime the only solution is to put them out on the streets... Or put them all in prison? Or put them into a nice zoo or something... A little ghetto all to themselves, where they can shoot themselves full of drugs and die without anyone noticing.

PROFESSOR: No, for goodness sake, that's not what I mean at all. I agree – a civilised society can't just ignore what's going on, can't just watch our kids dying in the toilet of some street-corner bar.

HEALER: Let's face the facts. This smug, self-satisfied, so-called civilised society only sits up and takes notice of drug addicts when the kids start making trouble for them. You don't hear ministers and newspapers and bleeding-heart liberals getting all worked up over the thirty thousand alcoholics who die every year of cirrhosis of the liver, do you...? That's because they have the good manners to die unobtrusively. If drug addicts died like old-age pensioners do – of poverty, loneliness and cold – nobody would say a word, would they! The thing about these kids is that they steal, and they dirty up parks with their syringes, and they go out and prostitute themselves... and since ninety per cent of them are HIV positive they're probably going to infect you with Aids too! And then they come and die right under your window! Their deaths create a scandal... They're an embarrassment. They are the bad conscience of our society! So prison is the only solution.

POPE: Exactly! You've hit the nail on the head! It's all hypocrisy, self-interest and intolerance. I like what you're saying, there... Professor, how about a massage? I don't think I can manage like this for much longer.

HEALER: Alright, let's see what we can do. Could someone take the gentleman's jacket off.

[*She begins to give him a massage.*]

POPE: But seeing that you provide this stuff more or less free, doesn't it ever occur to you that you're actually pushing young people into drug-taking? Those same young people who today are kept away from drugs precisely by the fear of ending up in prison...

PROFESSOR: ...and more particularly by the difficulty of getting hold of the stuff.

HEALER: I can see you're completely out of touch, Professor... You think it's hard to get the stuff! Ha! You see how the kids are laughing?

SECOND GIRL: That's right... These days heroin grows on trees.

FIRST GIRL: You can get the stuff any place and any time you like.

FIRST BOY: All you need is the money.

POPE: All right. Fair enough... But what about you...? Who gives you all this heroin? I presume it doesn't grow on trees.

SECOND BOY: We've already told you, Holy Man.

Every day somebody sends us between thirty and fifty doses and we don't have the first idea who.

PROFESSOR: What do you mean, you "don't have the first idea"? You must know who sends the stuff.

HEALER: No! We don't know. I presume we've got a hidden benefactor who wants to keep his identity secret. Anyway, every time it arrives in a different manner! One time someone comes shooting past on a motorbike and throws the packet through the door... Another time there's a pigeon comes in through the big broken window up there... with a packet tied to its leg.

POPE: A drug-dealing homing pigeon?

HEALER: Yesterday somebody sent us in two-dozen eggs... [*She points to one of the BOYS.*] This idiot didn't realise that two of them were stuffed full of heroin... He made us an omelette. Three grammes of heroin in an omelette! We ate it... You should have heard the burps afterwards... Deafening!

POPE: Do you really not know who sends you the stuff?

HEALER: No, honestly.... Every day the stuff arrives in a different manner... and in fact today, as you know, it came via you.

POPE: Exactly. Just call me Father Christmas!

HEALER: Anyway, how are you feeling now?

POPE: A bit better, thank you, but I still can't move my arms.

HEALER: I think I know how I could solve your problem once and for all.

POPE: How?

HEALER: Hypnosis.

POPE: Oh no you don't... I don't think so...! You'll have me going round on all fours and barking like a dog.

[*The door at the back of the stage opens with a big crash, and everybody turns round. Enter DRUNKARD. The Healer's ASSISTANT rushes to prop him up before he falls over.*]

DRUNKARD: I'm thirsty... I've come for my ration!

ASSISTANT: No problem. Come on in.

DRUNKARD: [*He disentangles himself from the ASSISTANT.*] I can stand up on my own... [*To the HEALER.*] Hey, Missus... where's my wine? [*To everyone.*] Your health!

CHORUS: Your health!

HEALER: Your health! [*To the POPE and the PROFESSOR.*] One of our regulars.

PROFESSOR: You don't mean you serve alcohol too...?

HEALER: We do our best to oblige. He's always here to get his ration, regular as clockwork: two or three litres at a time, and off he goes, drunk as a lord.

POPE: I'm impressed.

HEALER: [*She goes over to the DRUNKARD.*] Good day, my friend. What can I serve you? What do you fancy today?

DRUNKARD: I fancy something with a bit of a zing to it... a nice little Bulgarian Sauvignon, maybe. Pre-Chernobyl preferably.

HEALER: No problem. A very good vintage, too... I'll bring it up straight away... Straight from the cellar... But first, would you please look at my finger.

DRUNKARD: Why, what's wrong with it?

HEALER: Don't ask questions and just watch carefully... There it goes... round, and round, and round...

POPE: [*To the PROFESSOR.*] What's she up to?

PROFESSOR: I think she's trying to hypnotise him.

HEALER: There, well done... Now you feel all light... as if you're floating... you just stay like that... Good! Now, as a reward, I'll give you your cool fizzy Sauvignon. Here's the bottle... [*She mimes taking a bottle.*] You, take the cork out. [*She passes it to the DRUNKARD.*] I think one should have a tall glass for a Sauvignon.

[*She mimes polishing a glass.*]

DRUNKARD: Correct!

[*Having taken the cork out of the imaginary bottle, he pours himself a drink... He takes a sniff at it, and then drinks.*]

HEALER: How is it?

DRUNKARD: Good... Slightly fruity... Excellent! [*To the POPE and the PROFESSOR.*] Do you fancy a drop?

PROFESSOR AND POPE: No, no thanks.

DRUNKARD: The drinks are on me. It's my birthday!

HEALER: It's true. Every day's his birthday. You can't not accept a drink. Here are your glasses... [*To one of the GIRLS.*] Give us a hand.

[*They put on a performance of handing round glasses, pouring the wine, and drinking it. The POPE still has his arms up in the air. One of the GIRLS mimes handing him a glass.*]

CHORUS: Your health!

DRUNKARD: What do you think of my wine?

PROFESSOR: Good colour.

POPE: A touch fruity...

DRUNKARD: Down the hatch... This'll put hairs on your chest!

HEALER: Your health!

POPE: It's incredible – you actually use hypnosis to convince him that he's drinking?

HEALER: That's nothing... One time I even managed to convince a gentleman that he was throwing children out of a window... But that's another story.

PROFESSOR: But can you really cure him with hypnosis?

[*As if it's the most normal thing in the world, they all continue miming drinking.*]

HEALER: Of course... He's drying out a treat. Up until a week ago, he was miming up to four bottles a day... Now he's down to two!

DRUNKARD: Your health!

EVERYONE: Cheers!

[*The DRUNKARD heads off towards the exit.*]

PROFESSOR: Have you never thought of trying to use hypnosis with your drug addicts too?

HEALER: No. It can't be done. I've tried it. It's like trying to hypnotise a mirror.

DRUNKARD: See you, folks, that's all for today! Cheers!

EVERYONE: Cheers!

POPE: Maybe I'll live to regret this... but while you're at it, why don't you try hypnotising me too?

HEALER: All right... sit down here...

[*She points to a chair.*]

EVERYONE: Here's to it!

[*Enter two ARROGANT TYPES, pushing the DRUNKARD before them.*]

FIRST ARROGANT TYPE: Mind if we come in? How's business?

POPE: More drunkards?

SECOND ARROGANT TYPE: Any chance of a score at this time of day?

DRUNKARD: You can't come in. This is a private club.

FIRST ARROGANT TYPE: Shut up, you little prat!

[*They knock him over.*]

FIRST GIRL: You pigs!

SECOND GIRL: [*Going over to the ARROGANT TYPES.*] Who do you think you are?

[*The FIRST ARROGANT TYPE gives her a kick; the DRUNKARD gets up and leaves by the door.*]

PROFESSOR: What do you want?

HEALER: Are you looking for something?

FIRST ARROGANT TYPE: All depends on what you're offering. Who's in charge here? Are you Elisa?

HEALER: Yes, that's me... What do you want?

SECOND ARROGANT TYPE: Pleased to meet you. We're from the health authorities. Ha, ha...

[*He looks over at one of the BOYS, who is rubbing his arm, and then at the syringes on the trolley.*]

FIRST ARROGANT TYPE: That's nice. Looks like we've caught you red-handed. [*He grabs the BOY by the chin.*] Look at them all, all drugged up to the eyeballs.

SECOND ARROGANT TYPE: [*He uses his thumb to push back one of the GIRLS' eyelids to examine her pupil.*] Exactly. Look at their pupils. The size of pin-heads...

HEALER: So? What's it to you?

FIRST ARROGANT TYPE: Look, lady, like I said, we're from the health authorities. I think it would be useful if we had a look at the stuff you're using, just to check it for purity...

HEALER: There's no need to check it... We have the Professor here, he'll vouch for it.

PROFESSOR: Yes, I can vouch for it.

FIRST ARROGANT TYPE: Professor, eh? Professor of what?

PROFESSOR: Neuro-psychiatry.

FIRST ARROGANT TYPE: Oh yes? Well, I'm a specialist in advanced orthopaedic surgery. [*He grabs one of the GIRLS by the arm and forces her to the ground.*] And if you don't produce the goods pronto-pronto, I'm going to break this one's arm, and then I'll stick it in plaster... for free, ha, ha...

POPE: Leave that girl alone at once. You are rude, arrogant and intolerable, that's what you are!

SECOND ARROGANT TYPE: And who might you be? What's he doing with his arms up in the air, like he's saying "Hallelujah"?

FIRST BOY: He's a Hindu holy man. I think he's probably doing penance.

SECOND ARROGANT TYPE: Well, you just carry on with your Hallelujahs and don't interrupt, because otherwise I might just be tempted to kick you where it hurts!

POPE: Oh dear... I think I'll go back into my alcove.

[*The FIRST ARROGANT TYPE twists the GIRL's arm. She screams.*]

FIRST ARROGANT TYPE: Either you talk, or I'll break her arm! Where's the stuff?

[*The GIRL screams again.*]

HEALER: Stop it! Leave her alone. I've got the stuff. It's here... [*She hands the GANGSTER a couple of small packets.*] There you are. And I hope you die.

FIRST ARROGANT TYPE: This is just chicken-feed.

SECOND ARROGANT TYPE: What do you take us for, a couple of canaries? A little nibble just to keep us happy?

FIRST ARROGANT TYPE: What we're looking for is the Christmas cake... I think you know what I mean?

SECOND ARROGANT TYPE: That's right. We've developed a terrible appetite all of a sudden. Where's the stash?

HEALER: I'm sorry, but there's no Christmas cake here, and no stash either.

SECOND GIRL: It's true. The stuff comes in every day, but never more than fifty doses at a time.

HEALER: And we don't have the first idea where it comes from.

PROFESSOR: It must be a present from someone.

SECOND ARROGANT TYPE: A present?

POPE: A kind of miracle.

FIRST ARROGANT TYPE: Who asked you, Guru?

POPE: Well, to tell you the truth, I didn't believe it either, at the start, but it seems it arrives in all sorts of unexpected ways. One time somebody turns up on a motorbike... another time it's a pigeon with a packet tied to its leg. Then somebody else turns up and says: "Here you are, here's two dozen eggs." This cretin makes an omelette with two eggs full of heroin. Had everyone burping all over the place...

FIRST ARROGANT TYPE: Listen, Hindu... Either you stop taking the piss or I'll take your arms and ram them down your throat. In fact, do me a favour, put them down, will you, they're starting to get on my nerves.

POPE: I'm sorry, I can't. I'm a bit sort of seized up.

FIRST ARROGANT TYPE: Did I ask your opinion? Put them down, I said... They're getting on my nerves! In fact they're just about to make me extremely annoyed!

PROFESSOR: No, really, he's telling the truth. He really can't put them down. He's got what we call crucifixion syndrome, and witch's stroke.

POPE: That's right. I've got sciatic neuralgia, hyper-aesthesia, a sympathetic doo-da and a malfunctioning of my ganglia.

SECOND ARROGANT TYPE: Malfunctioning of the brain, that's what you've got. And now I'd say you're taking the piss.

FIRST ARROGANT TYPE: Correct! Put those arms down, and spare us the Hallelujahs... If not, I'll blow your brains out. [*He pulls out a big pistol.*] In fact how would you fancy some dental rearrangement? [*He puts the barrel in his mouth.*] I'm going to count to three... One!

HEALER: But it's true! He can't move... He's been like this for days!

SECOND ARROGANT TYPE: You can shut your mouth, too! [*He pulls out a gun, and points it at the HEALER.*] You'll see, he'll put them down soon enough...

FIRST ARROGANT TYPE: OK, now get those arms down... Two!

[*Everybody on stage shouts in unison:*]

ASSISTANT: Put them down!

FIRST BOY: Bring them down!

SECOND BOY: Do as he says, Holy Man, put them down!

THIRD GIRL: Down!

FIRST GIRL: Get your arms down!

SECOND GIRL: Hurry up!

FIRST ARROGANT TYPE: Bear in mind that when this gun goes off, it'll need a very big cork to plug the hole that's going to be made in the back of your head! Two and a half!

[*Everybody shouts:.*]

CHORUS: Nooo!

FIRST BOY: Don't be silly – get them down!

SECOND BOY: Get those hands down!

FIRST GIRL: Get them down!

THIRD GIRL: Down, for God's sake!

SECOND AND THIRD GIRLS: Down!

POPE: Aha! [*He lets out a yell, and then suddenly lowers his arms.*] They're down!

CHORUS OF YOUTHS: Amazing! He's done it!

POPE: Amazing, I've done it!

HEALER: Well done!

PROFESSOR: It's incredible, it worked!

FIRST ARROGANT TYPE: You see, Holy Man... ha, ha...big gun heap powerful medicine!

POPE: Uh uh!

[*As if a spring has gone into action, all of a sudden the POPE's arms go up again.*]

CHORUS OF YOUTHS: Oh no!!

FIRST ARROGANT TYPE: So – you want to play games, eh?

[*He points his gun again. The POPE very rapidly returns his arms downwards.*]

HEALER: Goodness, what an action!

PROFESSOR: How do you feel...?

POPE: Good... Better than hypnosis, this...

[*He moves his arms, waves them around, and generally flexes them.*]

HEALER: It's a bit drastic as treatments go... But it seems to work wonders.

FIRST ARROGANT TYPE: Right, that's enough of the chit-chat. [*To the HEALER.*] You, spit it out! Where's our stash?

HEALER: With the amount that people like you handle in a day, I don't see why you get so upset about an odd fifty doses? What's it to you?

FIRST ARROGANT TYPE: You think fifty shots a day is peanuts, eh? Day in, day out. Week after week. Anyway, it's the principle that counts... You're setting a dangerous example.

SECOND ARROGANT TYPE: Correct. People have started setting up centres like this in other parts of town, and that means the bottom's dropping out of our market.

POPE: Well, fancy that, I'd never have believed it...

FIRST ARROGANT TYPE: So we have to stop your nonsense before you get started! Understand?

HEALER: Perfectly... We're setting a bad example. Because we're ruining your market. [*To the POPE.*] Understand?

[*The SECOND ARROGANT TYPE pushes to front-stage a dressmaker's clothes rail on wheels. On it are hanging various garments, including a motor-cycle helmet and two carabinieri dress-uniforms complete with carabinieri hats with big feather plumes.*]

SECOND ARROGANT TYPE: Hey, look what I've found...!

FIRST ARROGANT TYPE: What's that?

SECOND ARROGANT TYPE: Look! [*He takes two police uniforms from the coat rail.*] And there's more where those came from... hats, boots, everything... Does this remind you of something?

FIRST ARROGANT TYPE: That's right! The people who held up our van were dressed as policemen! Well, isn't life amazing! [*To POPE and PROFESSOR.*] And, of course, you don't have the first idea what we're talking about...

PROFESSOR AND POPE: Er... no!

SECOND ARROGANT TYPE: *And* you play the dummy! To think that you almost had me fooled...

[*The two ARROGANT TYPES go over to the POPE and the PROFESSOR, holding the two police uniforms.*]

HEALER: What on earth has got into you now?

FIRST ARROGANT TYPE: Shut up, a minute. [*To the POPE.*] Put this jacket on for a minute, will you?

POPE: Why's that?

FIRST ARROGANT TYPE: Do as I say, or I'll blow your head off! Get a move on!

[*While the POPE is putting on one jacket, the SECOND GANGSTER forces the PROFESSOR to put on the other. Then they put the hats on their heads.*]

FIRST ARROGANT TYPE: Look at that – the jacket fits him like a glove... And the hat could have been made for him.

HEALER: Would you mind explaining what this is all about?

FIRST ARROGANT TYPE: Well, my dear Lady Bountiful, about a month ago a courier sent by our Calabrian friends was unloading a load of heroin from a van. A big load. Fifty kilos, in fact.

SECOND ARROGANT TYPE: Did you get that? Fifty kilos of Grade A, top-notch heroin.

FIRST ARROGANT TYPE: And all of a sudden, just like the movies, up jump four Rambos dressed like policemen, and, hey presto! They arrest his stash.

HEALER: Carabinieri in full dress uniform with feathers in their hats? What on earth are you talking about? These two look more like something out of Pinocchio!

FIRST ARROGANT TYPE: There was also another person, on a motor bike, and he had a helmet on his head that just happened to look exactly like this one. [*He puts it on. Then he takes it off and puts it back.*] Anyway, like I was saying... it could have been people from outside our patch... eh? A bunch of bastards like our friend the Guru here, for example, and his gang. In fact, the more I look at him, the more I have this feeling I've seen him somewhere before... Now where might that have been...? I reckon you *are* part of the gang. I think we can even prove it. I think we'll take a closer look at you.

SECOND ARROGANT TYPE: That's right. Up till now I'd say you've been taking us for a ride... But now *you're* the one who's going on a ride... Right, let's have you. Roll your sleeves up. [*To the HEALER.*] You, give him a hand... [*To one of the GIRLS.*] And you, take his shoes off...

POPE: What are you going to do with me?

FIRST ARROGANT TYPE: We want to find out if our Guru friend is on drugs. Hey, you, bring that bowl over here... and wash his feet... I want to see them clean.

[*The SECOND GIRL does as he says.*]

HEALER: I can assure you, this gentleman's not on drugs.

FIRST ARROGANT TYPE: I'm not so sure... [*To the HEALER.*] Oi, Mary Magdalene, get on with the washing...

SECOND ARROGANT TYPE: [*He inspects the POPE's feet.*] Nope, no signs of any needle marks.

FIRST ARROGANT MAN: Clean as a whistle. And look at those white feet! Could almost be an intellectual.

SECOND ARROGANT TYPE: That's good... that means it'll work even better...

HEALER: What d'you mean? What will work? What are you going to do?

FIRST ARROGANT TYPE: [*He prepares a hypodermic.*] Sit him down a bit higher... on that ledge... You'll see. We're going to have a bit of fun! We're going to give him a little shot of something...

PROFESSOR: Of heroin?!

POPE: Heroin?!

FIRST ARROGANT TYPE: That's right. But mixed with Pentothal. That way we'll have him singing like a canary on speed.

PROFESSOR: But you can't... That's very dangerous...

POPE: ...very dangerous...!

FIRST ARROGANT TYPE: [*To the PROFESSOR.*] Maybe you're right. You say you're a Professor? Well, that's nice, you can do it, then. Let's see how you get on with it.

[He hands him the hypodermic.]

SECOND ARROGANT TYPE: *[He points the pistol at the PROFESSOR.]* Go on, get a move on!

POPE: No! You can't! I won't have it! God Help Anyone Who Injects Me!

HEALER: You bastards! How can you...

[The FIRST ARROGANT TYPE hits her.]

PROFESSOR: I'm sorry, but I don't think I've much choice...

POPE: But what's going to happen to me afterwards?

FIRST ARROGANT TYPE: Oh, you'll be fine, Holy Man... You'll suddenly get this wonderful urge to talk, and you'll tell us all about your life, from when you were a little boy... And what you want to do when you grow up... and more particularly, what happened to our stash.

POPE: No, I don't want to!

FIRST BOY: Do it to me instead... I'll talk!

HEALER: Shut up, stupid!

POPE: *[Disentangling himself.]* No, I refuse to go along with this! You'll have to kill me first!

SECOND ARROGANT TYPE: Hey, the Holy man's playing hard to get! All right... Why don't we start with killing one of these junkies...? Let's see if that loosens him up a bit, even without the injection.

HEALER: I'm afraid this time they're not joking.

PROFESSOR: You'd best let them do it. It won't be too terrible.

POPE: I thought you just said it was very dangerous...!

FIRST ARROGANT TYPE: Right, we'll start with this one... *[He grabs one of the BOYS.]* And the rest of you down on your knees, because your turn's coming next. *[He yells.]* On your knees!

[All the DRUG ADDICTS go down on their knees.]

POPE: All right, all right... I'm ready. Do the injection! They're closing the hole in the ozone layer, and they make up for it by making a hole in me!

FIRST ARROGANT TYPE: Ah, at last! *[To the PROFESSOR.]* You – get on and do the injection. *[The PROFESSOR carries out the injection, assisted by the HEALER.]* Now shut up all of you, and sit still. As from this moment, God help anybody who utters a word, because you might put the Guru off and blow his fuses. I'm the only one who's talking, alright?

POPE: *[Speaking with difficulty.]* Who's that...? Where are you...?

PROFESSOR: There, it's starting to take effect. I'd advise you to keep your questions general to start with... take it very, very gently.

FIRST ARROGANT TYPE: All right, no problem. Right, Mr Guru, can you hear me. Nod your head if you can hear me... *[The POPE nods his head.]* Are you there? Right now, tell me, what's your name?

POPE: I don't remember...

FIRST ARROGANT TYPE: The kids here tell me your name's Holy Man.

POPE: Holiness, actually...

FIRST ARROGANT TYPE: Is that your first name or your surname?

POPE: Er. Surname.

FIRST ARROGANT TYPE: So what's your first name?

POPE: First name... er... His... His Holiness...

FIRST ARROGANT TYPE: Holiness, His, His, Holiness... whose Holiness... Very odd, this... And I suppose it's your pals who call you Guru...?

POPE: No, not Guru! Not a Hindu! I'm not called Guru. I don't have anything against Hindus, but I'm not called Guru...

FIRST ARROGANT TYPE: OK, not Guru... Just His Holiness the Holy Man. Now, you know a thing or two about drugs, don't you?

POPE: [*Still speaking with difficulty, but gradually loosening up.*] Do you mean heroin?

FIRST ARROGANT TYPE: Yes. Tell us everything you know.

POPE: Yes... everything I know. I aam reeady n-o-o-w. Heerooin iis ca-a-alled Anita in street slang...

FIRST ARROGANT TYPE: Anita?

POPE: That's right. Anita in the sense of Anita Garibaldi, wife of the great Italian hero, his companion in all his adventures... and therefore a heroine herself, so to speak...

FIRST ARROGANT TYPE: [*Laughing.*] Hey, I like it! Carry on!

POPE: Heroin – or Anita – costs two dollars a gramme at the start. But by the time it gets to Europe, where it's refined, the price goes up to fifty dollars a gramme... and then, after it's been cut, the price per kilo...

SECOND ARROGANT TYPE: We know, we know: a kilo brings in something like two hundred million, and that stash that you hijacked must have been worth at least ten billion.

PROFESSOR: Please... don't interrupt him... If you do he might go off the rails.

FIRST ARROGANT TYPE: Precisely... [*To the SECOND ARROGANT TYPE.*] You behave yourself... I'm the one asking the questions...

POPE: Problem: If one gramme of crude heroin costs fifty dollars at the start, how much will a kilogram of refined heroin cost once it is refined, if its value is increased by one thousand times during the refining process? That's your homework for tonight...

FIRST ARROGANT TYPE: We can do without the wisecracks, Holiness. As you were saying: "At the start, fifty dollars a gramme..."

POPE: That's right, highly profitable. One of the most profitable businesses there is. A big market... big stakes, but a big pay-off...

SECOND ARROGANT TYPE: Hey, listen to the Hindu! He's not as stupid as he looks.

FIRST ARROGANT TYPE: Shut up!

POPE: The profits from drugs are invested...

SECOND ARROGANT TYPE: [*Irritated.*] Woah, that'll do... You're not addressing a conference, you know... Ask him who he works for.

POPE: ...in the building industry, producing profits of the order of...

FIRST ARROGANT TYPE: Stop a moment... Would you mind saying who you work for?

POPE: For the Vatican.

FIRST ARROGANT TYPE: For the Vatican?

SECOND ARROGANT TYPE: He's taking the piss again.

FIRST ARROGANT TYPE: Well, it's not so odd when you think about it. You read the papers, don't you? You must have heard of the Sindona case, and Sindona's links with the Vatican, via Cardinal Marcinkus? And what about that Judge Ambrosoli who was killed?

POPE: Marcinkus, Sindona, Calvi. Calvi used to go to London quite regularly, and by way of entertainment he used to do balancing tricks under Blackfriars Bridge. So that he could maintain a perfect balance he would always keep two bricks in the left pocket of his coat, and a very heavy briefcase in his right hand... And in order not to get a soaking in the smelly waters of the Thames, he used to put a rope round his neck. Oh dear, he slipped, and ended up hanged... The bricks in his pocket were found... But not his briefcase! Weird, eh? Vanished! Problem: Where did Calvi's briefcase end up? That's your homework for tonight...

FIRST ARROGANT TYPE: Get on with it, Mr Guru... Whose idea was this joke about free drugs?

POPE: The Vatican's...

FIRST ARROGANT TYPE: The Vatican?

POPE: Yes, the Vatican.

FIRST ARROGANT TYPE: And who organised the raid on the van?

POPE: The Vatican.

FIRST ARROGANT TYPE: The Vatican again?

POPE: Yes, the Vatican.

SECOND ARROGANT TYPE: Here we go again! If you ask me, the needle's got stuck...

POPE: The Vatican.

FIRST ARROGANT TYPE: [*To the PROFESSOR.*] Give him another shot. Maybe he's running out of juice.

PROFESSOR: But I've already given him an entire syringe-full... I have to protest. This really is very dangerous... And anyway you run the risk that he's going to clam up completely...

FIRST ARROGANT TYPE: Pump away, pump away!

[*The HEALER does as he says.*]

POPE: [*He continues, in the tone of a radio announcer.*] A spokesman for the US State Department has stated that it is unlikely that the Mafia and the international drug cartels are ever going to be defeated by military means.

FIRST ARROGANT TYPE: That's better. That's got him going again.

POPE: The only way to eliminate them is to liberalise the entire drug market, under the control of the state.

SECOND ARROGANT TYPE: Uh oh... I don't like the sound of this... Where the hell's he taking us now?

POPE: President Bush developed the point further, in his latest speech to the American people, when he admitted that repression only brings about a development of the drug market, and an increase in the number of deaths...

SECOND ARROGANT TYPE: Hey, slow him down a bit. He's starting to blow his fuses.

FIRST ARROGANT TYPE: Right! Listen, Holy Man, can you hear me? Hello, is anyone there?

POPE: [*As if on a telephone.*] Yes, I hear you... It's His Holiness here... Hello... Hello... Put another coin in, please. Thank you!

SECOND ARROGANT TYPE: Yes, hello! Can you hear me? Right, Holy Man, now, tell me from the beginning, who set up this business about free dealing? Whose idea was it? Don't just tell me the Vatican. I want names.

POPE: It's a crazy Utopian idea...

FIRST ARROGANT TYPE: Yes, agreed, but we want to know the name...

POPE: The only trouble is, there'll be a terrible fuss if this ever gets out.

FIRST ARROGANT TYPE: Why? It must be someone pretty important. Who is it?

POPE: The Pope.

FIRST ARROGANT TYPE: Which Pope?

POPE: *The* Pope. [*He points to himself.*] His Holiness the Pope.

FIRST ARROGANT TYPE: What – the Pope?

POPE: That's right. It was like a miracle. For so long I was blind. Then, all of a sudden, my eyes were opened. Now I see things as they really are.

FIRST ARROGANT TYPE: Correct me if I'm wrong, or is he talking like he's the Pope?

PROFESSOR: Ah yes... Classic split personality syndrome.

HEALER: He's identifying with the Pope.

SECOND ARROGANT TYPE: Oh for God's sake...!

POPE: No, I don't think it's to do with God... This time God doesn't come into it. Or yes, maybe it was God who inspired me. My ganglia seized up because I had hardened my heart... The real blockage was not in my nerves but in my brain... The fires of my human action were extinguished because there was nothing alight in my spirit...

FIRST ARROGANT TYPE: Oh God! He's giving us the Pentecost sermon!

SECOND ARROGANT TYPE: That's all we need – he's going ga-ga.

FIRST ARROGANT TYPE: Shut him up, for fuck's sake! Professor, either you turn him off somehow, or I'll turn him off with this.

[*He waves his pistol.*]

PROFESSOR: Well I don't quite know where to start.

HEALER: Let me have a go. [*She takes up a position in front of the POPE.*] I'll pretend I believe him... You have to give him a bit of leeway... If he thinks he's the Pope, then the only way to deal with him is to talk to him as if he is the Pope. [*She changes tone, and takes him by the hand.*] Your Holiness, can you hear me?

POPE: Eh? Somebody call? Who's there?

HEALER: It's me... the missionary nun from Burundi... Remember?

POPE: Ah yes... The children... A hundred thousand children in St Peter's Square... Am I still there? Oh my goodness yes! Look at them. Thousands of them! They're climbing up! Quick, get a stick, knock them off...!

HEALER: Don't let them get too close! Remember the black-eyed beans!

SECOND ARROGANT TYPE: They're all raving mad!

POPE: All squashed! But one was saved!

HEALER: Yes – poor Little Pea. Saved by hiding in a thimble!

POPE: Poor Little Pea, stuck in there with all those beans...

HEALER: OK, OK, that'll do...!

POPE: That's a shame... I remember the whole story, you know!

HEALER: Save it for later. These gentlemen are getting a bit nervous, and they want you to tell them the truth about the raid on their stash.

POPE: The raid on the Calabrian van... with Pinocchio and the policemen?

HEALER: That's right. Well done. Why don't you tell it from the beginning?

POPE: [*Speaking in a steady rhythm.*] Yes, yes... Well... Once upon a time, in the police station, there was a talking cricket... a mole, in fact... or to be more precise, a talking cricket-mole.

FIRST ARROGANT TYPE: What mole, what cricket? I want names.

POPE: I'll talk... I'll tell everything.

[*The HEALER makes other gestures. The POPE accelerates to a high speed. At that moment the door at the back of the stage is flung open. The two GANGSTERS spin round, guns at the ready. Enter the DRUNKARD.*]

DRUNKARD: Relax, friends! Make yourselves at home! The drinks are on me!

SECOND ARROGANT TYPE: Hey, Drunkard! I came within an ace of shooting you! Where do you think you're going?

[*The DRUNKARD wanders off on an exploration of the premises. The two GANGSTERS follow him. The PROFESSOR takes advantage of their absence to mutter to ELISA.*]

PROFESSOR: Am I mistaken, or did you just hypnotise him...? Was it you making him say all that stuff?

HEALER: After all that heroin and Pentothal he was very open to suggestion.

PROFESSOR: What about the bit about the bogus policemen, and the raid on the drugs van...

HEALER: All true. If you must know, the robbery was organised by some of our friends.

PROFESSOR: So they're the ones who send you your daily doses.

HEALER: We're opening quite a few centres like this one and the bottom's dropping out of their market. Shush, they're coming back...

[*The DRUNKARD reappears, followed by the two GANGSTERS.*]

DRUNKARD: Here we are again.

FIRST ARROGANT TYPE: Right, you, sit there, and don't interrupt! Let's get on with it.

[*With a gesture from the HEALER, the POPE continues talking, but this time in a normal rhythm.*]

POPE: Thanks to the mole, we knew exactly the route that the goods were going to take, and we knew the exact day and time when the van was going to be transporting the stuff...

FIRST ARROGANT TYPE: This is wonderful, Holy Man. Go ahead, you're doing well!

POPE: [*All of a sudden he changes tone.*] Ha, ha, ha! Faroes, Dogger Bank and German Bight, visibility down to one mile...

SECOND ARROGANT TYPE: What in hell's name is he talking about now?

HEALER: It's the shipping forecast. He's jumped channels! [*Annoyed.*] It's your fault. You put him off his stroke with all your yakety-yak. Why can't you just keep quiet!

POPE: Um... Fungal growths of green algae are suffocating the fish. Bishops are calling for special prayers to be said...

FIRST ARROGANT TYPE: Switch channels! Why can't you get him to switch back again?

HEALER: Hey, go easy, he's not one of your super-modern portables, you know. He's a bit of an antique.

POPE: Try Carynthia, the double-action tampon for the woman with an energetic life-style! [*He changes rhythm and voice.*] Haha! A problem with bad breath? Try Resolax... Works under your armpits too. [*He changes tone again.*] At an industrial court in Turin, the FIAT motor company has been on trial for its record of accidents and industrial injuries. The judge has ruled that managing-director Romiti is innocent of all charges. The blame rests entirely with the workforce, because for years they have been deliberately pushing their arms and legs into the company's machinery, thereby seriously threatening productivity.

DRUNKARD: I think that's enough telly for today. Anyone fancy a beer? The drinks are on me...! [*He mimes handing round the glasses.*] Bottoms up!

FIRST ARROGANT TYPE: Drunkard, I'm going to kill you.

DRUNKARD: No, my dear Arrogant Man... You're not going to kill me, no!

FIRST ARROGANT TYPE: Yes, I shall shoot you, if you carry on interrupting... I shall shoot you in the head!

DRUNKARD: Really?

FIRST ARROGANT TYPE: You can count on it!

[*He pulls out his gun.*]

DRUNKARD: OK, let's see who's quickest on the draw! [*He goes through the classic gunslinger routine. He spins round and pulls an imaginary pistol out of an equally imaginary holster. He reaches out and points with two fingers as if to shoot; then he mimes putting the gun back.*] OK, cowboy, I'm ready... Are you?

FIRST ARROGANT TYPE: [*Seriously shaken.*] I'm going to kill you for real, now!

CHORUS: Noooo!

HEALER: Leave him alone... He's just a drunk!

PROFESSOR: Yes... What good would it do you to kill him?

[*The FIRST ARROGANT TYPE pulls out his pistol. The DRUNKARD reaches out his arm all of a sudden and points his finger. A shot is fired. The GANGSTER touches his head with his hand. A trickle of blood runs down from his forehead. He takes his hand away, and we see a bullet hole.*]

FIRST ARROGANT TYPE: Oh no!

[*He slumps to the floor.*]

SECOND ARROGANT TYPE: But who fired?

DRUNKARD: Who do you think? ...Me!

SECOND ARROGANT TYPE: With your finger?!

DRUNKARD: That's right. This finger never misses... Truth to tell, the finger acts only as a gunsight... The actual gun's up my sleeve here. [*He pulls up his sleeve to reveal his arm, where he has a kind of track attached to his forearm.*] Look, here's the gun. No handle – it doesn't need one. The gun runs down this rod. Invention of mine... Clever, eh? When I reach out like this, the gun runs down... and... bang!

[*We hear another shot.*]

SECOND ARROGANT TYPE: [*Putting his hand to his stomach.*] You... bastard...!

[*He slumps to the floor.*]

POPE: End of transmission. And, as the Bible says: "Blessed are those who shoot first... for they shall be the last to reach the Kingdom of Heaven."

[*Blackout.*]

[*Musical interlude.*]

SCENE 2

[*The big traverse with the painted fresco comes down, and we are in the corridor facing the POPE's apartments. Enter the FIRST CARDINAL, with some newspapers in his hand, followed by two PRIESTS, who periodically raise small transistor radios to their ears.*]

FIRST CARDINAL: Oh, it was terrible! You should have been there... The crowd was devastated...

FIRST PRIEST: How did he begin?

FIRST CARDINAL: Nothing at all... He went out on the balcony, rolled up his sleeves, showed his bare arms and said: "Look, I too have taken drugs!"

FIRST PRIEST: Incredible! And how did the crowd react?

FIRST CARDINAL: People were fainting... People were crying... Some people were jeering... Most people didn't understand.

FIRST PRIEST: Well, I suppose it's a bit provocative on his part, but it could end up positive in the end.

FIRST CARDINAL: What do you mean, positive? A Pope who says that we should be nice to drug addicts... And try to understand them... And that we should love them as our dearest children. I tell you, it's a scandal! In fact, it's like the end of the world has broken out! And now we've got journalists invading by the thousand... And a sea of camera crews from every television company in the world, even Japan.

SECOND PRIEST: [*Removing the transistor radio from his ear for a moment.*] The government's fallen!

FIRST CARDINAL: But we knew that this morning.

SECOND PRIEST: No, I'm talking about the American government... [*He puts the radio back to his ear... And then takes it away again.*] And the German government.

FIRST CARDINAL: This is incredible! Never heard anything like it!

FIRST PRIEST: [*Listening to the radio.*] The Christian Democrats have split down the middle... The German Christian Democrats are in a major crisis... The Jesuits have gone into liquidation...

FIRST CARDINAL: You see! What was that you were saying about "positive"?

[*Enter the PROFESSOR.*]

PROFESSOR: Here I am... What on earth is going on?

FIRST CARDINAL: Oh, at last!

PROFESSOR: I came as quickly as I could... But why all the panic, what's going on?

FIRST CARDINAL: You really mean to say that you haven't heard?

PROFESSOR: I've been in the operating theatre since dawn this morning. I left somebody's brain open in the hurry to get here.

[*Enter the HEALER, in a hurry. She is dressed as a nun, but on her feet she wears a very visible pair of red high-heel shoes. She is also carrying her two large bags.*]

HEALER: What on earth is all the fuss about?

FIRST CARDINAL: Ah, that's good, you're here too...

HEALER: You made me come in such a hurry... I'm all out of breath! I couldn't find my nun's outfit... Apart from which, I was halfway across St Peter's Square before I realised that I hadn't changed my shoes... These are the shoes that I wear to go out dancing on Saturday nights... I had to cross the square like this... [*She bends her knees so that her nun's habit covers her shoes.*] And everyone was saying: "Look at that dwarf nun... with the red shoes on!" [*To the PRIESTS.*] Would you mind getting me a chair? I'm completely worn out! [*One of the two PRIESTS exits, and returns immediately, carrying a stool.*] Why on earth is it that every time I come to the Vatican I have to put up with this bordello... [*She corrects herself.*] er, I mean... this crowd... this very big crowd!

FIRST CARDINAL: I think you had the right word the first time. Every time you show up, it's a disaster.

HEALER: Watch what you're saying, Cardinal, I'm in a right mood for a punch-up.

FIRST CARDINAL: Ah, I see. So you don't think you're the main one responsible for this disaster?

HEALER: Me?!

FIRST CARDINAL: Who was it put all these ideas into the Holy Father's head, and got him all worked up, so that now he's going round like a man possessed?

HEALER: I suppose, the next thing, you're going to stick me on a bonfire and burn me as a witch!

FIRST CARDINAL: That's it! Witch! Just the word I was looking for!

HEALER: Your Eminence, why do you feel this need to treat me so badly? Why do you have to keep picking on me? Look at me, I've had to run all the way here... I'm half out of breath... And you still start having a go at me. You've been treating me terribly ever since Act One... Why can't we stop arguing, and make friends. Look, I've brought you a present.

FIRST CARDINAL: What's that?

HEALER: [*She pulls an abacus from her handbag.*] Here you are. For the next papal elections... Seeing that your Vatican computers are always breaking down.

FIRST CARDINAL: You're a witch!

PROFESSOR: Hey, go easy, your Eminence.

FIRST CARDINAL: [*Launching into the PROFESSOR.*] It's all your fault. You brought her along in the first place. [*To the HEALER.*] Now, do me a favour, will you? Let's have the Holy Father back like he was before.

HEALER: In other words, crippled with paranoid delusions about children climbing up the front of St Peter's with balloons?

FIRST CARDINAL: Exactly. I think we'd rather have him suffering all the nightmares of Saint Anthony the Hermit, rather than have him raving round like a demented paranoiac, like he is now!

HEALER: Will you just listen how this man talks about his Pope!

FIRST PRIEST: Yes, if you'll permit me, Your Eminence, I believe that the apparent madness which seemed to have seized the Holy Father is, in truth, a sign of God's will, and that, furthermore...

FIRST CARDINAL: Shut up... Creep!

PROFESSOR: Excuse me, might I know what horrifying catastrophe our Holy Father is supposed to be responsible for now?

FIRST CARDINAL: An encyclical!

PROFESSOR: An encyclical? And what could be so paranoiac and demented about an encyclical?

FIRST CARDINAL: In this instance everything's paranoid and demented. For a start, the title: "Heroinum et Omnia Medicamenta Stupefactiva..."

PROFESSOR: Heroinum et Omnia Medicamenta Stupefactiva?

FIRST CARDINAL: "..et Potionem Psicotropicae Libera Sunto."

PROFESSOR: "Libera Sunto"?! An evidential accusative indeed! Is that how the encyclical starts?

FIRST CARDINAL: Yes, look, have a read...

[*He passes him a newspaper.*]

PROFESSOR: I'm afraid I left the hospital in such a hurry that I forgot my glasses.

HEALER: You probably left them in your man's open brain. Never mind. I'll read. "Heroinum et Omnia Medicamenta blah-di-blah. The Pope has initiated a campaign for drugs to be distributed at affordable prices by all national governments."

PROFESSOR: A liberalisation of drugs?! So he's taken you literally!

FIRST CARDINAL: Precisely... It was you who put this criminal idea into his head, and now you're going to have to sort him out again! Understand?

HEALER: Do you mind if I continue, Cardinal? "The Pope has taken up the proposal of the bishops of Sicily, and has promised excommunication for all drug traffickers, in particular the Mafia, and all those who support them or cover up for their criminal actions. Immediately, three ministers and eight under-secretaries in the Italian government declared themselves Muslim. The Church is being torn apart. Schism is the order of the day. The bishops are in revolt. The entire Dutch and Brazilian clergy are with the Pope. A general Synod has been called for today. The more conservative elements in the American and European clergy have decided to elect an anti-Pope. The French tend towards Lefebvre, while the Italians bishops are favouring Donat Cattin...

PROFESSOR: I don't believe it; this is incredible!

FIRST CARDINAL: Slow down, that's not the end of it!

FIRST PRIEST: [*With his ear to the radio.*] Listen to this!

SECOND PRIEST: [*Also with the radio to his ear.*] What frequency are you on?

FIRST CARDINAL: That's not the end of it! The second part of the encyclical is all to do with unplanned pregnancies and unwanted children, and needless to say with contraception.

HEALER: The Pope really goes to town here. He says: "We should not see a condom as the Devil's raincoat...! Similarly, the contraceptive coil is not some centrifugal device invented by the Devil, designed to make the spermatozoa so dizzy that they can't go about their business!"

[*Exit the two PRIESTS.*]

PROFESSOR: He's the first Pope in history with a sense of humour!

FIRST CARDINAL: Sure, but things have reached such a pitch that the Catholic Youth Federation have decided to remove the Pope's statue from all their branch offices, including the Catholic University, and have replaced him with statues of Andreotti and Craxi, holding hands.

[*We hear a warbling tone. The CARDINAL answers his mobile phone.*]

FIRST CARDINAL: Hello? [*He listens, and then replaces the phone, and announces:.*] That was to tell me that the Holy Father is arriving!

[*Enter the FIRST NUN, followed by two SWISS GUARDS, and the CAPTAIN.*]

FIRST NUN: Make way for the Holy Father!

[*Everybody stands back. The CAPTAIN OF THE GUARD looks round suspiciously.*]

CAPTAIN: [*Pointing to those present.*] Search them!

[*The GUARDS begin to search FIRST CARDINAL, the PROFESSOR, and the HEALER.*]

FIRST CARDINAL: Get your stupid hands off...! I'm the Pope's personal secretary!

CAPTAIN: I'm sorry, orders from above!

[*Enter the POPE, accompanied by a short FRIAR.*]

POPE: [*To the CAPTAIN OF THE GUARD.*] No, no, they're alright... I can vouch for them... [*To the PROFESSOR and the HEALER.*] How goes, my friends? [*Pointing to the CAPTAIN.*] You have to understand, a short while ago someone tried to shoot me. [*They all look at each other in alarm.*] A bullet came in through the window. Bang! Missed my head by two inches.

[*Once again, reactions of alarm.*]

FIRST CARDINAL: This must be the response to your threat to excommunicate the Mafia.

POPE: You think so...?

[*He walks round the room, closely accompanied by the FRIAR and the SWISS GUARDS.*]

HEALER: No, I don't think the Mafia's too upset about the excommunication... They're a law unto themselves.

POPE: Yes, I don't think the Mafia comes into it either. I think we're dealing here with religious fanatics... As a friend of mine once said: "I prefer criminals to idiots. Because criminals take a rest every once in a while... but idiots, never!"

PROFESSOR: You've caused quite a stir, your Holiness!

POPE: That was exactly what I intended! Did you like my encyclical?

PROFESSOR: Very courageous!

HEALER: A broadside, Holy Father!

FIRST CARDINAL: Exactly. Just like the real ones they'll be firing off any minute.

POPE: Why do you always have to be such a pessimist? Anyway, it's not over yet. Tomorrow I'm coming out with a supplement to the encyclical, which should raise a few hackles.

HEALER: What is this, a serialised encyclical?

POPE: Don't joke. I'm serious! Listen: "The Church must become poor again, as it was at the beginning, and must impose upon itself a dignified poverty!"

FIRST CARDINAL: Dignified blooming poverty!

POPE: All the Church's goods will be distributed to those in need. All bank accounts of the various religious orders and bishoprics will be abolished. All the Catholic banks will be required to reorganise by law, which will force them to be totally open about their dealings.

FIRST CARDINAL: Open about their dealings? Excuse me, Holy Father, but this means suicide... We're coming up to the year 2000, and you want to plunge the Church back into a pauperist Middle Ages running alive with pre-Waldensian fanatics and Anabaptists!

POPE: Am I right in thinking that you just called me a fanatic?

CHORUS: [*With extreme amazement.*] The Pope a fanatic?!

HEALER: Don't pay any attention, your Holiness. I'm sure you're going to hear worse... Anyway, if I may be allowed, from this moment you're going to have to watch yourself. Everyone from the Mafia on downwards is going to be queuing up to take a pop at you.

POPE: You mean you don't think I'm careful enough already? Already I have to go round surrounded by hordes of people to protect me. You can't imagine how this dear Friar here [*He points to the small FRIAR.*] pursues me. He doesn't leave me alone for a minute. He tastes all my food for me... And everything I drink... Starting with my coffee. I go to take a sip of a cup of coffee... He grabs it and just about swallows the lot...! Call that a taste? And then it has to be without sugar, because that's the way he likes it... Then I wait for a moment to make sure it doesn't have a Sindona effect on him, and then at last I get to drink myself. [*He goes and sits down, with his back facing off-stage left.*] I tell you where I draw the line, though – using the same toothbrush – that's going *too* far! [*We hear the dull thud of an explosion.*] What was that?

CAPTAIN: The explosion came from your rooms, Holy Father!

[*The CAPTAIN exits, followed by the SWISS GUARDS.*]

POPE: From my rooms?

[*He gets up, and as he walks across stage we see that he has an arrow stuck between his shoulder blades.*]

PROFESSOR: What on earth is that?

POPE: What? Where?

PROFESSOR: In your back... There's an arrow sticking out of your back.

POPE: Well, fancy that! I didn't even notice! [*To the little FRIAR.*] You're not guarding me very well behind! [*To everybody.*] Luckily I was wearing an orthopaedic corset, and that stopped the arrow.

PROFESSOR: Are you still wearing the corset?

POPE: Yes, just as a precaution... in case I get struck rigid again...

[*The HEALER plucks the arrow from the POPE's back.*]

PROFESSOR: Excuse me a moment.

[*He exits.*]

POPE: I wonder who fired the arrow.

HEALER: [*She studies the arrow.*] I'd say it was a
Comanche arrow...

POPE: Comanche?

HEALER: Calabrian Comanches!

[*The PROFESSOR re-enters, with the SWISS GUARDS
and the CAPTAIN. They are carrying a NUN, who is
dying.*]

POPE: What happened?

CAPTAIN: The canary in the cage. It exploded just as she
was about to give it something to eat.

HEALER: A canary bomb?!

PROFESSOR: They replaced your canary with a
mechanical canary stuffed with TNT... All it needed
was for the Sister to nudge it... and Bang! Here's all
that was left.

[*He shows some feathers.*]

POPE: Of the Sister...?! Oh no, the Sister is there. [*The
PROFESSOR exits, following the SWISS GUARDS, who
carry the dead NUN.*] It's usually me who feeds the
canary... He used to peck it out of my palm. He never
was very good at it. Look at the state of my hand!

FIRST CARDINAL: Well, I would say a prayer of thanks-
giving would be in order, your Holiness!

POPE: Yes, I suppose it would.

[*Enter the CAPTAIN, running. He is listening to a walkie-
talkie.*]

CAPTAIN: Look out, your Holiness. I've had a report that a small radio-controlled car has been spotted. It's apparently heading this way, from the south wing. It might be a bomb!

FIRST CARDINAL: Quick, find somewhere to shelter... Get out of the way... The thing could be stuffed with dynamite.

POPE: South must be that way...

[*Everybody follows him.*]

PROFESSOR: No, no, South is this way.

POPE: Well in that case we have to run that way.

[*The big traverse with the fresco rises. We see the same scene as in Act One (The interior of the POPE's apartments). The walls of the previous stage setting have been pushed back, so that what we see is pillars and arches that create a sequence of quadriporticos. A structure which is open to the sky. All of a sudden a model car appears and zigzags at speed across the stage. The actors rush hither and thither trying to escape it.*]

POPE: There it is! It must be a Lebanese toy!

HEALER: Ha, they think of everything!

[*She jumps out of the way.*]

FIRST CARDINAL: [*Leaping about.*] Stop it! What are you waiting for?

PROFESSOR: A miniature car-bomb! What is the Vatican coming to?

POPE: [*Also leaping out of the way.*] It's like being in a miniature Beirut! A Lebanese Euro-Disney!

CHORUS: It's going to blow up! It's going to blow up!

[*The little car continues racing around. They all leap about and change positions in a strange kind of dance, to the insistent rhythm of a Mozartian toccata and fugue. Every now and then the vehicle stops. The music also stops and everyone on stage stops moving. Then they start up again, matching the speed and the movements of the miniature car-bomb. This action is not overplayed but is played at more or less normal pace. Then the car comes to a complete halt. It lets out a menacing hiss. From its dashboard a jet of smoke emerges... Everyone begins to cough. The POPE is coughing so badly that he is bent double.]*

PROFESSOR: It's gas! What a stink! Get that thing out of here!

[A SWISS GUARD does as he says.]

POPE: [*Coughing.*] I'm suffocating!

FIRST GUARD: Here, your Holiness... It's aromatic ozone, compressed... one hundred per cent pure!

[He hands him an air cylinder, with a mouthpiece to breathe with.]

POPE: Thank you...

[As he is about to put the mouthpiece to his mouth, the small FRIAR grabs it from his hand.]

FRIAR: No, your Holiness! I have to try it first!

POPE: Oh, don't be such a fuss-pot!

[The FRIAR puts the mouthpiece to his mouth and breathes deeply.]

PROFESSOR: How is it?

FRIAR: Nice! Like bitter almonds with a touch of smoked kipper.

PROFESSOR: Like Dioxin! Don't breathe it!

FRIAR: Too late!

[He slumps to the ground.]

HEALER: Well, look at that, he's stone dead!

POPE: This is murder...! I feel ill...!

HEALER: The *Catholic Herald* strikes again!

FIRST PRIEST: [*Listening to his transistor radio.*] Incredible... The Queen of Holland has supported the Holy Father's statement about liberalising drugs.

POPE: That's good news!

FIRST CARDINAL: Oh go on! That's impossible!

FIRST PRIEST: [*He turns up the volume on his radio, so that everyone present can listen.*] Listen!

ANNOUNCER'S VOICE: The governments of Denmark, Ireland, and Sweden, along with the Belgians and the Austrians, are expected to vote on the proposal shortly...

FIRST PRIEST: [*At the window.*] Oh, look, your Holiness. What an amazing sight! There are thousands of them!

POPE: Thousands of whom? Where?

HEALER: Down in St Peter's Square... Seminary students, monks, nuns... Young people from the Catholic Youth Organisation... All gathering to hear what you have to say.

POPE: Oh, so I've not ended up as isolated as some people were trying to make out.

[*He points to the FIRST CARDINAL.*]

PROFESSOR: You must be joking, your Holiness... You have reawakened such a passion, such a commitment... especially among the Catholic youth. Listen how they're calling for you.

HEALER: They're full of feeling for you!

PRIEST: You're going to have to go out and address them, your Holiness...

FIRST CARDINAL: You must be joking! It would be

madness... First, from a political point of view... I know what they're doing, they're trying to draw us into a schism in the church! And secondly, there's the danger of snipers... who, I'm sure, will be hiding on the terraces and statues out there...

PROFESSOR: That's impossible. Out on the terraces there are hand-picked marksmen from the Vatican's security services.

HEALER: That's exactly what worries me.

CAPTAIN: [*He walks confidently over to the window.*] No, no, you can trust them. [*We hear a rifle shot.*] Not too much, though.

[*He falls to the ground, dead.*]

POPE: He's dead! This is terrible!

PROFESSOR: Stay back, your Holiness. Get down!

FIRST CARDINAL: [*Pointing outside.*] Did you see... It was one of your hand-picked Vatican marksmen!

HEALER: Hand-picked, but blind! He must have mistaken the Captain's helmet for the Pope's mitre!

[*The CARDINAL's mobile phone rings. He takes it from his pocket.*]

FIRST CARDINAL: Excuse me, someone's calling. [*He answers his portable phone.*] Hello? Yes, of course... I'll be down at once... [*To the POPE.*] I'm sorry, but I'll have to go down... It's urgent... If you'll excuse me, your Holiness. [*He exits.*]

POPE: Yes, yes... see you later. Have you noticed how that one absolutely doesn't care at all. I hope his walkie-talkie blows up in his pocket! [*The two NUNS carry over a silver sculpted bust on a small pedestal, so that the POPE can shelter behind it.*] May Saint Callisto protect me!

HEALER: Listen, that sculpted portrait of you over there has given me an idea...

[*The PROFESSOR exits.*]

POPE: You're thinking of putting it out on the balcony in my place?

HEALER: Exactly... But we'd need a volunteer to hold it up...

POPE: A volunteer? A kamikaze merchant, more like. He'd be a sitting duck.

HEALER: We'll find one, your Holiness.

[*She runs off stage. The PROFESSOR re-enters, holding the sculpture of the POPE.*]

PROFESSOR: Here it is.

SWISS GUARD: [*To the PROFESSOR.*] Get down!

[*We hear a shot.*]

PROFESSOR: [*He walks bending forward for fear of being hit by a bullet.*] And I've also got a piece of good news for you. Your poison-tester is better already... And here he is...

[*Enter the small FRIAR.*]

FRIAR: Here I am!

SWISS GUARD: Get down!

[*The FRIAR ducks down, and only just in time, because we hear a shot.*]

POPE: Oh, I am glad...

[*Enter the HEALER, carrying a long papal tunic.*]

HEALER: And here...

SWISS GUARD: [*To the HEALER.*] Get down!

[*We hear another shot.*]

POPE: Goodness, what a lot of shooting! It's like being at the Yacht Club in Naples.

HEALER: [*Bending double.*] And here I've got your tunic. [*To the MONK*] Brother Monk, you who have just been saved from death... Would you be willing to put on the Pope's head, and the Pope's tunic, and be Pope in the place of the Pope? [*The MONK shakes his head vigorously.*] He said yes. Well done, thou good and faithful monk!

POPE: Thank you, you are too generous. But wait... At least let us take some precautions. First you should wear a breastplate underneath... [*To the SWISS GUARD.*] You...

SWISS GUARD [*He comes over.*] Your Holiness?

CHORUS: Get down!

[*The SWISS GUARD ducks.*]

POPE: You'd better give him yours. In fact, go over there and help him to put it on.

PROFESSOR: It would be best if you put on a breastplate and helmet as well, your Holiness. Come over here, I'll help you into the ones that the Captain was wearing, the one who was shot.

POPE: Won't that be terribly unlucky, though...? Oh alright, I'm coming... But I'm bringing my bronze Saint with me as a shield... [*Raising his voice as he shouts out of the window.*] There's no point in you shooting, I'm protected by a Saint. [*A loud shot is heard.*] Formigoni! I saw you with that gun!

[*The PROFESSOR and the POPE exit back-stage.*]

[*Enter the HEALER, the SWISS GUARD, and the FRIAR dressed as the Pope. The young FRIAR has put on the armour. He has the sculpted head of the Pope above his own head, wearing the Pope's mitre. He is also wearing the Pope's robes.*]

HEALER: [*To the NUNS.*] Could you give me a hand...?
[*The NUNS lift a big icon down from the wall and carry it
to front-stage.*] Get down! [*The entire group takes shelter
behind it.*] Now, Brother Monk, you have to step out
onto the balcony. Raise your arms in the way that the
Pope does... And in the meantime, the Holy Father will
speak through the microphone from back there... [*The
FRIAR has by now completed dressing up as the Pope.*] How
do you feel?

[*The din increases. Enter the PROFESSOR.*]

CHORUS: Get down!

[*Another shot is heard.*]

PROFESSOR: Goodness, listen to all that shouting down
there! Are you ready with the dummy?

[*At this point a BRAZILIAN NUN enters and throws
herself to her knees before the animated puppet.*]

BRAZILIAN NUN: Oh, your Holiness, finally I meet
you!

SWISS GUARD: [*Trying to stop her.*] You can't... You have
to ask for an audience first... You can't just...

BRAZILIAN NUN: [*Extricating herself.*] Oh, most holy
Father... I am a poor nun from Brazil... Here, prostrate,
in order to express my gratitude...

PROFESSOR: No, I'm sorry... His Holiness is rather busy
at the moment...

BRAZILIAN NUN: I have come to thank the Holy
Pontiff on behalf of our Indian brothers, because with
his encyclical he has...

HEALER: Listen, Brazilian nun! Calm down for a
minute! The Pope has to show himself to the people
from the balcony now! Wait till he's...!

BRAZILIAN NUN: [*She pulls out a gun and pushes the*

SWISS GUARD aside.] Right then, show yourself to the people... dead...! [*She shoots the DUMMY in the chest.*] You red Pope, you communist, die!

[*She shoots the two NUNS, the SWISS GUARD and the PROFESSOR. They all fall to the ground. Then she points her gun at the HEALER.*]

HEALER: Not me, I'm nothing to do with it...! I just happened to be passing.

BRAZILIAN NUN: You don't fool me... You must all die! [*She fires at the HEALER, but her gun jams.*] Putana de mierda! I'm out of bullets! [*She hurls down her gun, takes the mitre off the DUMMY's head, puts it on her head, and runs to the window.*] He's dead! The Pope is dead!

[*We hear a shot. The BRAZILIAN NUN falls to the floor, dead.*]

HEALER: Everyone dead here? [*To the PROFESSOR, who is lying on the floor.*] How goes, Professor?

PROFESSOR: [*Raising himself.*] Fine... Fine...

[*The POPE enters, dressed as a Captain of the Swiss Guards.*]

HEALER: [*To the POPE.*] Get down!

[*We hear a shot.*]

POPE: It's terrible... All these people dead... All on my account...! And me, the one they want to kill, I'm still alive!

PROFESSOR: It's a shame we can't say as much for these poor monks and nuns.

HEALER: [*She pulls aside the garments concealing the small FRIAR.*] Your poison-taster has copped it too, poor thing... Fancy that, dying twice in the space of ten minutes! The Brazilian shot him through the head... His head, unfortunately.

POPE: Oh my God, so he sacrificed himself for me twice! I told you he was a persistent little beggar.

[*Enter two BLACK FRIARS, wearing hoods and bearing a catafalque. On it they place the body of the FRIAR, who is still disguised as the POPE.*]

HEALER: Such is the price of faith!

POPE: No, we can't carry on like this, with people getting shot... Take off that contraption he's wearing... Get those clothes off him.

HEALER: No, your Holiness. Do as I say. Don't take the clothes off... Leave him dressed as the Pope... And you must stay dressed as a Swiss Guard.

POPE: But who's ever going to believe that I'm Swiss?

HEALER: You make a perfect Swiss.

[*Enter a HOODED MONK, with a briefcase. He turns to the disguised POPE.*]

HOODED MONK: Are you Swiss?

POPE: Jawohl... Schweitzer.

HOODED MONK: From Bern?

POPE: Ja, von Bern...

HOODED MONK: [*He hands the briefcase to the POPE.*] A man called Carboni asked me to give this to you.

[*He exits.*]

POPE: Carboni...? It's the briefcase! It's Calvi's briefcase!

HEALER: Throw it away!

POPE: No, those documents could be a bombshell!

HEALER: Throw it away!

[*The POPE throws the briefcase off stage. We hear a big bang, accompanied by a flash and smoke.*]

POPE: I told you so...!

[*Enter the FIRST CARDINAL.*]

FIRST CARDINAL: Is it true, what people are saying?!
[*The POPE, still disguised as the CAPTAIN, moves to back-stage.*] Have they really shot the Holy Father?

HEALER: Brown bread, I'm afraid. He's stopped
breathing...

FIRST CARDINAL: [*He hurls himself on the body of the
Pope's DOUBLE.*] He's icy cold... There's blood... He's
dead! [*He runs to the window and calls out.*] The Holy
Father has been killed... He's dead! They've killed the
Pope! He's dead!

[*He runs off, shouting.*]

POPE: Don't say that! I'm alive... Wait...! [*The FIRST
CARDINAL carries on shouting offstage.*] There's no
telling some people...!

HEALER: [*Stopping him.*] No, let him go and spread the
news.

POPE: The news that they've killed me? Why's that?

HEALER: Do as I say. For the moment it's best you let
everyone think you're dead.

[*Enter the FIRST CARDINAL, SECOND CARDINAL,
and a THIRD CARDINAL, followed by MONKS and
NUNS wearing capes and black hoods; they carry four
candles, which they arrange at the four corners of the bier.
At the foot of the bier a number of cushions are placed, and
around it three large seats.*]

SECOND CARDINAL: Oh, what a terrible thing to
happen!

THIRD CARDINAL: A crime against humanity!

FIRST CARDINAL: The Lord is putting us to a terrible
test!

CHORUS OF ALL THE BYSTANDERS: Examina nos pretende dei!

SECOND CARDINAL: But how did it happen?

THIRD CARDINAL: Who killed him?

HEALER: Well, what happened was that...

FIRST CARDINAL: All right, that'll do... You can tell us afterwards.

[*The CARDINALS go to kneel on the cushions.*]

SECOND CARDINAL: Post tempora melior nunca sapere.

THIRD CARDINAL: Why has the hand of God struck so hard?

CHORUS: Te acclamabit pater et fulgitur fuit.

SECOND CARDINAL: Orridum eliamos... Such a thing is unprecedented in the history of the Church...

THIRD CARDINAL: ...for a Pope to be killed...

FIRST CARDINAL: No, no, you're wrong... It has happened... It happened before...!

SECOND CARDINAL: Yes, it's true... But with those pontiffs you could almost say that they deserved...

THIRD CARDINAL: Yes, in fact you could say those particular deaths were a liberation for the Church.

FIRST CARDINAL: But this one... a martyr...

THIRD CARDINAL: A martyr, so eager for his martyrdom!

SECOND CARDINAL: Well, yes, I suppose he did rather go looking for it.

CHORUS: Deus gratia acclamabunt!

[*The CARDINALS seat themselves on the thrones.*]

SECOND CARDINAL: When all's said and done, it was the hand of the Lord that called him to him...

HEALER: Yes. I've often heard the Mafia referred to as the "Hand of the Lord".

THIRD CARDINAL: What was that, Sister...?

HEALER: And the Camorra, I suppose, could be the "Touch of the Holy Ghost"!

CHORUS: Laude, laude... in gloria tuam!

SECOND CARDINAL: The problem is, we don't understand the logic behind all this...

PROFESSOR: [*Coming from backstage.*] Look what I've found – a bug.

[*He displays a small gadget.*]

FIRST CARDINAL: A what?

POPE: An acoustic bug... You know – a spy microphone.

FIRST CARDINAL: A spy microphone?

PROFESSOR: Yes, and I found another one hidden in his phone.

[*He shows another, which is even smaller.*]

HEALER: It's obvious that somebody has been watching and checking on the Holy Father's every movement.

FIRST CARDINAL: And now that you've unplugged the Pope... I mean, unplugged the microphone...

CHORUS OF CARDINALS: The Pope is no longer of any use.

FIRST CARDINAL: The spy bug is no longer of any use!

CHORUS: Exaude gloria nos... Alleluiah!

HEALER: Microphones in every bit of plasterwork...! It's like being in the Sicilian Law Courts in Palermo.

CHORUS: Nunque intendemus.

[*From the square we hear the growing noise of a big crowd.*]

FIRST CARDINAL: Listen to the noise they're making.

SECOND CARDINAL: [*Muttering to himself.*] Hooligans! Trouble-makers! They're agent provocateurs, that's what they are! [*To the CAPTAIN/POPE.*] You, Captain, go down and disperse them by force...

POPE: The force of a full company, your Eminence?

FIRST CARDINAL: Certainly, there must be two or three hundred thousand people out there!

POPE: If you don't mind my saying so, it was a mistake not to give us Swiss Guards tanks... a hundred or so... nice big heavy ones...

FIRST CARDINAL: No, no, for goodness sake, moderation is always our best weapon... We have to be political... give and take... choose the middle option... Be diplomatic with people.

CHORUS: Utque versum stracere.

[*The FIRST CARDINAL calls for a censer, and swings it so that it emits clouds of incense.*]

SECOND CARDINAL: We shall begin a process of beatification of our Holy Father here!

CHORUS: Sanctus, sanctus... Petrus et Pauli fuerunt!

THIRD CARDINAL: Of course, it will take time.,..

SECOND CARDINAL: We should not be in too much of a hurry...

CARDINALS: [*In chorus.*] Tempore probi et savi sunt.

CHORUS: Promittere et transigere.

CARDINAL: [*In chorus.*] Dilatare e distendere... Rinviare et eludere.

FIRST CARDINAL: There will have to be a transitional period... Then a pause before the Conclave...

[*He hands the censer to the THIRD CARDINAL.*]

THIRD CARDINAL: The Conclave will be a difficult one...

SECOND CARDINAL: A lot of black smoke...

FIRST CARDINAL: But in the end a new Pope will be chosen... A Pope who is wise, mild-mannered... and maybe even a teensy bit poorly...

POPE: Oh yes, of course, the best popes are always the popes who don't last long... In fact the best popes die more or less straight away.

CARDINALS: [*In chorus.*] Captain! Such language! At a moment like this!

THIRD CARDINAL: Is that a proper way to talk of our Holy Martyr?

POPE: What do you mean, martyr...? He was an extremist. A fanatic... a complete lunatic! How could anyone in their right minds imagine dismantling the Mafia... with all the interests that are involved... and the power balances that rely on it?

FIRST CARDINAL: Well, yes, of course, it was rather Utopian... But...

POPE: Utopian, you call it... Politics, economics... finance... All blown sky-high... Millions of workers employed in drug-trafficking and the recycling of drug dollars... all sacked... Not to mention hundreds of subsidiary firms all going to the wall. Hundreds of useless empty mouths waiting to be fed... Old people living longer than they need to... Millions of blacks invading Europe...!

FIRST CARDINAL: Yes, yes, we agree, it was madness, but this is no language to be using!

CHORUS: Verbum molestus deprecamus!

POPE: [*Aggressive, in a Slavic grammelot.*] Ma vadoona meschiskaia vescvia... vadoons chia cabrimka!

[*He snatches the censer and starts whirling it over the CARDINALS' heads.*]

FIRST CARDINAL: What did he say? What's got into him?

CHORUS: Ellitur conficere!

THIRD CARDINAL: What on earth are you saying?

POPE: Eascariosia steroma alunca cardilala... brumbuania!

SECOND CARDINAL: I think he's insulting us!

CHORUS: In mescula intrisus calamus!

POPE: Ummelia kauschia – ebey paradoe avaschiaira!

FIRST CARDINAL: What are you saying, Captain?

POPE: Ayusca vineschiana!

THIRD CARDINAL: What's the meaning of all this?!

FIRST CARDINAL: Potens amelita! Who gave you permission to interfere like this?

POPE: Stariota ameschima mechinaia!

[*By now he is giving free rein to his Slavic grammelot.*]

CARDINALS: [*In chorus.*] He's mad! What's got into him?

POPE: [*He continues in grammelot.*]

CARDINALS: [*In chorus.*] Help! Who do you think you are?

CHORUS OF CARDINALS: It's the devil!

[*The POPE removes his Captain's helmet, takes the mitre*

from the sculpted head, and puts it on his own head; he goes and sits on the throne in the centre of the room, and raises his arms.]

POPE: [*In Latin grammelot.*] Astra umus suntum papam!

[*Everyone falls to their knees.*]

GENERAL CHORUS: The Pope has risen from the dead!

HEALER: Oh no... That's a terrible mistake, your Holiness!

PROFESSOR: You really shouldn't have shown yourself!

[*The POPE rises to his feet and sings in Gregorian Chant, a powerful Gloria. His singing is interrupted by a shot. The POPE stiffens for a moment, with his arms outstretched, and then falls backwards, dead.*]

HEALER: [*She comes to the front of the stage, with a missal book open in her hands.*] It really is true what Saint Augustine said: "Woe betide that man of power who takes the side of those who have no power."

[*The Gregorian chant becomes louder as the lights slowly dim.*]

THE END

Editor's note The Latin used here is dog Latin with no particular meaning.

THE FIRST MIRACLE
OF THE BOY JESUS

A comic monologue

TRANSLATOR'S NOTE

This comic monologue was written as a companion piece to Dario Fo's *The Tale Of A Tiger*, and he toured both pieces together in the early 1980s.

Both monologues were written in dialect – a created dialect of the Po Valley, which Fo has made his own.

There is by now a tradition that we translate Fo's plays into standard English. Performers and producers are invited to adapt the text to suit their local circumstances.

Ed Emery

THE FIRST MIRACLE
OF THE BOY JESUS

It was night... and through the great dark sky, full of stars, a fiery comet suddenly flashed. Like a bolt of lightning, with its blazing tail of fire... Zigzagging across the sky like a wild serpent, and plunging down among the shining stars. Like a bat scattering a huddle of frightened lizards... And those poor stars were scared. They shouted:

"What was that! For heaven's sake!"

And the great star staggered like a drunkard and moved off and disappeared into the distance, tracing a great trail, which, as it happened, was the route for the Three Wise Men. The Three Wise Men were three kings, who had come from afar, from the East.

The oldest of the Three Wise Men was a king with a big crown on his head, and white hair and a grey beard. His face was wrinkled, he had a terrible hooked nose, and he swore a lot. He swore because he had boils on his bum, and every time his horse went bump, they hurt, and he'd go "Nyaah... mutter, mutter, mutter".

The was another king. He was young. He rode a white horse. He had a crown on his head, and long, flowing golden ringlets. He had clear blue eyes. And he always had a smile on his face. Then there was another king. He rode a camel. He was a black king, so black that compared with him the grey camel that he was riding seemed whiter than the white horse of the blond king. He was handsome, always smiling, and when he rode his camel he always sang. Over and over again. And this is what he sang:

"Oh how fine it is, to ride on a camel!
Oh what a treat! Oh what a treat!
Bumpety-bump on the hump of a camel.
Oh what a treat to be on a camel, going to Bethlehem.

Under the light of a thousand stars,
With a comet guiding us
To the little hut
And to the Madonna who's singing lullabies
To the baby who's crying and whingeing.
And Saint Joseph, sawing his wood,
And the cherubim, flying and praying,
And the ox and the ass, snorting and braying,
And my camel trots along, bumpety-bump.
Oh it's great to ride on a camel!
It's a lot better
Than riding on a horse
Because a horse shakes your bollocks,
And this doesn't happen on a camel.
Oh what a treat! Oh what a treat!"

"Stop it, stop it!" spluttered the old king. "I can't stand it! Four days and four nights now, he's been singing about how wonderful it is on his bloomin' camel!"

[*The BLACK KING starts his ditty again.*]

"Obviously I'm going to sing,
Because it helps my camel to keep going,
Because if I don't sing,
The camel falls asleep.
And when he falls asleep, he trips up
And falls over right on top of me,
So I get squashed.
So of course I sing on my camel!
Oh what a treat! Oh what a treat!
And this way we get to the manger,
With the Madonna singing lullabies,
And Saint Joseph, sawing his wood,
And the baby, crying and whingeing,
And the cherubim, flying and praying.

The camel going bumpety-bump,
Oh what a treat! Oh what a treat!
You have to sing on your camel,
So as to give it a bit of rhythm,
Because riding a camel isn't like riding a horse,
Because a horse can gallop along,
But a camel goes bumpety-bump,
One paw in front and one behind,
And if you don't give it the right rhythm,
One leg gets tangled up with the other,
It trips over its toes,
And over it goes!
And I end up squashed by my camel.
Oh what a treat! Oh what a treat!
I'm off to Bethlehem on my camel.
OOOOOH WHAT A TREAT!
OOOOH WHAT A TREAT!"

"Stop it!" shouted the old king, in desperation. "If you don't stop, I'm going to skin you and eat you alive! I'll peel off the black, and I'll eat all the pink bits inside! I'll eat you whole!

"I ask you, what a daft idea, sending a black king along as well, just because all humanity had to be represented! Why didn't we bring a yellow one as well, or a red one, or a spotty one? No, he had to be black! And then he's got those white eyes, with the black pupil in the middle and when it's dark, they glow red and he looks like a wild animal.

"You know, the other day I went into a field because I had to see to my bodily needs... I pulled down my trousers (excuse me if I go into details), and there I was, halfway through, squatting on my haunches, just like this, when all of a sudden I see in front of me two eyes of some wild animal! I shat on my trousers! And then it turned out it was him, shitting right there in front of me! He was shitting, but he *wasn't singing*! The first and only time that he'd not been singing. At the very least he could have sung: 'Oh what a treat! What a treat to shit without your camel'!"

At that moment the comet star did a big swoop, like a meteorite, and came to a sudden stop in the middle of the sky.

"What's happened?"
The black king answered, with a little song.

"It's stopped to get its breath back!
That means we've arrived!
We've almost arrived at Bethlehem.
Oh what a treat! Oh what a treat!"

In desperation the old king spurred his horse and went galloping off like a madman, but the black king followed hard on his heels, and both of them disappeared off into the darkness and vanished... But even though you couldn't see them, in the distance you could still hear:
"Oh what a treat, oh what a treat!"
"Shut up!"
"Oh what a treat..."
"SHUT UP!"

[*He mimes listening to voices getting fainter and disappearing off into the distance.*]

"Oh what a treat...!"
"SHUUUUT UUUUP!"
And then came a great silence.

At that moment, all of a sudden, a great big angel appeared in the sky. His hair was ruffled and his locks were blowing in the wind. He had a gold halo fixed on his head. And great folds of silk clothing which billowed in the wind like loose-hanging sails. And across his chest was a big silk sash, with big letters saying: "Angel!" Just in case anyone hadn't noticed. And this angel, with his great big coloured wings, looked more like a flying pheasant. He came zooming down, skimmed the ground, and as he pulled out of his nosedive he shouted:

[*He mimes the ANGEL doing a nosedive to the ground.*]

"Men of good wiiiill... come, for the Redeemer is boooorn."

And all the shepherds threw themselves to the ground, terrified!

"Heeeey... Are you crazy? What are you trying to do, crush us? You've frightened all the sheep and now they won't give any milk."

[*He mimes another nosedive by the ANGEL, which comes within an ace of flattening the SHEPHERD who is speaking.*]

"I hope you end up crashing into the mountain, so's your halo jams itself down over your head, and all your feathers scatter far and wide. You great chicken!"

And the shepherds set off towards the manger, and they took with them all sorts of things to eat. Some of them took cheese, some of them a little goat, or rabbits, another took chickens, and another took wine and oil. One of them took baked apples, and tarts with chestnuts. And then there was one idiot who turned up bringing polenta *alla Bergamasca.* I ask you, giving polenta to a new-born baby! Anyway, they said:

"We have to make the crib!"

In the manger, Mary's mother, Saint Anne was arranging all the presents that people had brought. The manger was packed full of things to eat. The donkey was so buried under parcels and packages that you could only see his head, and the poor thing could hardly breathe.

The cow was completely covered, you couldn't see her at all. Chickens, cheeses, salamis, bottles everywhere... It looked more like a street-market! The Three Wise Men arrived, and they went down on their knees. There was the old king, who brought his gift; then the young king, who brought *his* gift; and then the black king arrived...

"Oh what a treat! Oh what a treat to see!
The baby in his cradle!"

"Out you go... black man! You'll frighten the Baby! If you must sing, sing outside!"

At that moment, they heard the noise of soldiers arriving. The soldiers were going from house to house to find out whether the Redeemer had been born, so that they could kill him. And lo and behold, the big angel suddenly arrived right in front of the house where the Madonna and Baby Jesus were, and he stood in front, with a huge sword. The soldiers got to the house, and the one leading them said:

"Stop. Look. In front of that house. A bloody great angel! Come on, let's go, before he splits us in half! Come on, let's get out of here!"

Now, at that very moment, stomp, stomp, stomp, a town crier arrived on the scene.

"Calling all mothers! Hear ye, hear ye! Whosoever of you has, within these three days, given birth to a child, may be happy, because the king has decided to give a prize to the most handsome baby in his kingdom. Bring your baby to the palace. Bring it to Herod's big house. The king will be the judge, and he will present the most beautiful baby with a little crown, with an inscription: 'What a beautiful baby! This baby is almost more beautiful than the Son of God!' And the woman who bore him, too, will have a crown, inscribed: 'This is the mother who gave birth to the beautiful baby!'"

Saint Anne heard all this, and immediately rushed to find the Madonna:

"Come on, they're giving a prize for the prettiest baby. Bring Jesus along."

"No, I don't want to. I don't need prizes or rewards. I'm happy just as I am!"

"No, the world should know about your baby. We can't have Herod's prize going to another baby! Come on, come on! Do as your mother says!"

They were just about to leave, when they had an idea:

"Wait a minute, we'll go and get some ribbons to make the baby pretty. Joseph, you keep an eye on him and make sure nothing happens to him."

They go out, and immediately Joseph stops sawing and says:

"There must be a trap here. I'm sure it's a trap, Baby Jesus. What do you think?"

And Baby Jesus, who was not daft, said:

"Yes, yes..." And he winked.

So Joseph pulled out a jam jar where he kept some black stuff for painting chains. He took a little brush, and tac, tac, tac, he put little black dots all over the baby's face, and the baby pulled faces, because it tickled.

"Now you just stay there!" And he carried on sawing.

When Saint Anne came back into the house:

"Waaah! Chicken pox...! Black chicken pox! It must have been that black man who came in frightening the baby!"

Saint Anne was a *Sun* reader.

But then she took a rag, and, wipe, wipe, wipe, she wiped the spots off, and the baby was all clean again.

"Somebody has been painting spots on our baby's face! I wonder who that might have been!"

Joseph carried on sawing:

"Hrumph. Don't ask me! Haven't a clue!"

"You there, with your silly saw, you'd better watch your step, because otherwise, I might decide to saw something of yours off!"

Saint Anne was a terrible woman!

Then she and the Madonna went out again, to get some ointment to put on the baby to make him smell nice.

"Now, watch out. We're going out, and you'd better mind that nothing happens to the baby, because we'll know who to blame if it does!"

When the women had gone out, Saint Joseph didn't know what to do... But then he saw a great big wasp sitting on the wall... all black and yellow stripes, a great big whopper of a wasp. He took a glass... and... whap! He used the glass to trap it against the wall... Then he took a bit of card, and slipped it under the glass. Caught it!

[*He mimes imprisoning the wasp in the glass.*]

"I'm sorry, but I'm going to have to give you a bite on the cheek. Whap! Whoomf! [*He mimes an immediate swelling on the baby's cheek.*] Now the other side. Whap! Whoomf! [*He mimes an immediate swelling on the baby's other cheek.*] Zap! And another on his forehead! [*He mimes as above.*] In the name of the Father...(etc)."

Then he returned to his sawing, carrying on as if nothing had happened. Saint Anne came back into the room:

"Aaaargh! God! Look at that! Waaah! What happened! What a monster! Look at the state of him!"

"Don't just stand there crying. They'll be gone soon, said Joseph. "Two months at the most."

"What's that?"

[*She points to one of the wasp stings.*]

"It's a wisdom tooth!"

"But there's one on both sides!"

"Yes!"

"And one on his forehead too!"

"Very wise baby..."

The Madonna started crying, and Saint Anne likewise.

"Oh, what bad luck! Why did he have to go and get three wisdom teeth today, when there was such a good prize to win! We won't be able to take him now, he looks terrible!"

A little while after, down the road, they heard the sound of crying. They heard the desperate screams of women, of mothers, carrying their babies, all bloody and cut to pieces.

"Waaah! It was a trap! No sooner were we in the courtyard than Herod shut all the gates. And soldiers came in and killed all the babies. It was a trap! All our babies, killed!"

So then Saint Anne realised what had happened, and went down on her knees. And the Madonna too. And both of them cried out:

"Thank you, God, thou who art so wise and all-knowing. With this clever device of the wasp stings, you tried to save this baby so that he would not end up in Herod's clutches. Aha! What intelligence! What a wonderful idea, oh Lord!"

And this rather irritated Joseph, and he sawed and sawed and sawed, sawing so hard that he even sawed through the bench that he was sawing on, and he spluttered:

"That's the way it is... Always like that! Every time!" he said. "A fellow has a bright idea, and everyone goes off thanking God, who never had anything to do with it in the first place!"

At that moment, an angel came in, crying:

"Out, get out," he said. "Flee the massacres!"

"What do you mean, the massacres?!"

"Time to move! Get out! You've got to run!"

"Where to?"

"The Flight into Egypt!"

"Already?"

"Yes, because there's all the soldiers outside, and they're looking for you."

"Wait, first we'll have to get a cart," said Saint Anne. "So that we can load up the presents that everyone's brought us."

"No presents. You're not allowed to take anything with you!"

And the Madonna said:

"Do you mind, young man! Presents don't grow on trees, you know. I want them for the baby, for when he grows up..."

"Bring out the donkey!"

"You must be joking," said Joseph. "You can't load up

that donkey. He's been going for four days and four nights, the poor thing's worn to a frazzle!"

And at that moment, the donkey came forward, walking like a drunkard. The poor creature could hardly stand, and as they loaded him his legs began to buckle. They loaded all the bottles, and the pots, they loaded the cheeses, and the parcels and the bundles. And all of a sudden, the poor thing collapsed. Whoomf, he went. His knees buckled, and his belly hit the ground. And there was the Madonna, still sitting on his back, with the babe in her arms.

"Madonna," said Joseph, "you're going to have to get off, because the poor thing can't budge. It's dying."

"But I can't, dear. In the *Flight into Egypt* the painters always show me sitting *on* the donkey."

So Saint Joseph got down underneath the donkey, and humped it up on his back, and off they all went. Then, after two days, or maybe three, the whole Holy Family arrived at Jaffa. The white city of Jaffa, with all its tall, wonderful towers.

And all at once the angel flew up into the sky, with a great swoop. And the donkey lifted up its great head. Brrrrrrr! [*He imitates the donkey farting.*] The donkey farted! Brrrrr! The donkey's soul went off to heaven. His legs splayed out, and, boomp, his belly hit the ground. And the Madonna, sitting on the poor expired beast, looked, and said:

"Poor thing! It must be a sign from God. It means we've arrived!"

They entered the city, and found a hovel, a rat-hole of a place, which made the manger in Bethlehem look like a palace. Joseph blocked off all the draughts with bits of cardboard, and the family settled down to sleep. Then, first thing next morning, the Madonna took a basket and went round looking for clothes to wash, because she had to find some way of supporting the family. And Saint Joseph went around with his hammer, his saw and his nails, to try and find a job. And the kid was left out in the street.

That evening, the Madonna arrived home dead-beat, tired and sweating and with her back all aching. Then Saint Joseph returned, furious, because he hadn't earned a penny all day. He sat down there, and with his hammer began to hit his fingers on the table! Whack! Whack! Whack! Whack! Because that's the way that carpenters like to let off steam. Then Baby Jesus came in, with snot hanging from his nose right down to his chin, his hair all over the place, his hands dirty, his trousers all crooked, and no shoes on his feet.

"Mum! I'm hungry!"

"Oh, that's lovely manners, that is...! You come home and instead of asking your mum and dad if they're alright, or if they're tired... Why do you have to be so horrible, eh?"

"But mum, I'm hungry!"

And the Madonna:

"You should be ashamed of yourself. Don't forget that you came from heaven especially, that you were born into the world to show others how to be good, and to show love, and to have good words for everyone... And here you are, with the first two Christians, to whom you should show some respect, and you don't even ask them how they are!"

The Madonna was furious. And Joseph too. They sat down at table.

"Boy, go and wash your hands. And wash your face too. And blow your snotty nose. Look at the state of your golden ringlets! Tidy them up a bit. And before you eat, make the sign of the cross. Oh no... wait... it's a bit early for that!"

Then the child went to bed. And the Madonna went to bed, and so did Joseph. In the morning, Jesus woke up, and he found himself on his own again. All alone, with no one around. So, he put on his trousers, ate a bit of bread, and went out in the street, and there he saw all the children playing: leapfrog, and hide and seek, and hopscotch...

"Hey, kids! Can I come and play with you?"

"No!"

"I'll be the leapfrog! Let's play leapfrog. And hopscotch!"

"No! Go away... Palestiney!"

"Let's play 'On it'. You can chase me. I'll be the robber. Can I be the robber?"

"No!"

"But why not?"

"Go away, Palestiney! Peasant!"

The boy started to cry. He cried with great big tears from his great big eyes. And at this point, just for a bit of fun and the chance to amuse himself with the other children, he did a miracle. Despite the fact that his mother was forever telling him:

"Don't go doing miracles around the place, because if anyone sees you, they'll realise that you're the Son of God... and then Herod's soldiers will arrive, and we'll have to run away again!"

In the middle of the square was a fountain. And all around the fountain there was red clay. The kind of clay they use to make bricks. Baby Jesus took a handful of the clay, and began to mould it with his little fingers. He made a bird's head, then the bird's little body, with little wings and tiny, tiny feathers. He took two twigs, to make its little legs...

"Look, look at this little bird I've made! It's made out of clay!"

"Oh well done, Palestiney! He comes all that way to show us how to make a clay bird... Oh brilliant, I don't think!"

"Yes, but I know how to make it fly."

"What do you mean?"

"I breathe on it."

"Let's see."

"Look! Whoosh!"

[*He blows on the bird.*]

And the little bird opened its wings, and stretched itself, and beat its wings: chirp, chirp, cheep, cheep!
[*With his hands, he mimes the bird flying around, and then disappearing off into the sky.*]

"Hey, that Palestiney is a genius! Brilliant! Hey! He made a clay bird, and then he made it fly, just by breathing on it. Made it out of clay..."

"I don't believe you."

"What do you mean? I saw it with my own eyes!"

"That trick's as old as the hills. He finds a little stunned bird that's fallen down from a tree. He picks it up. He dunks it in water and rubs it in the dust a bit. Then he cups it in his hands, blows up its bum... the bird gives a little shiver... chirp, chirp, chirp... and off it flies!"

"But no! I saw it! It really was made of clay! Come on, Palestiney, show us again! Come on, another bit of clay. Look, see, he's doing it... Give it its little wings... And now, blow!"

"Wait!"

"Who...?"

A big lad arrived on the scene, a boy with a big head, and long black curly hair.

"Hang on a minute. I want to take a closer look!"

"Who are you?"

"Thomas!"

"Thomas? That figures!"

[*He shrugs his shoulders, resignedly.*]

Doubting Thomas took a nail... and tack, tack, tack... He stuck the clay bird full of holes:

"All in order. Off you go!"

"Alright, now I'm going to blow!" [*He blows.*] Whoosh... cheep, cheep, chirp, chirp...

[*Once again, he mimes the bird flying off.*]

"It's flying! The bird is flying! Bravo, Palestiney! Hey, I like you! This is fun! Now everyone's going to make a bird. And then Palestiney will, whoomf, breathe on them, and make our birds fly!"

"Come on, Palestiney! You're brilliant, you are!"

And all of them began making birds. One of them made

a round peacock with a straight tail, and square wings and a great big head drooping forward. He put two feet on it. Crash... it fell over... So then he made it four legs, then five.

"You can't have a bird with five legs..."

"Well... it won't stand up otherwise... Anyway who cares, as long as it flies..."

Then another one made a kind of sausage thing, with twelve wings in a row, no tail, and twelve feet.

"It's a dog..."

Then another child made a big pastry thing which looked more like a jam tart, with a head jammed in the middle, no neck, a beak pointing up... and its wings all splattered out all around. And no legs.

"I don't know if that one's going to fly, we'll have to see..."

Then another kid made several little birds which looked like little turds. Another one made a great big turd. And the last one made a cat!

"You can't make a cat fly!"

"If that big turd there is going to fly, then my cat can fly too!"

"No, you can't make cats fly. That's not fair!"

"Mum! Palestine says he won't make my cat fly!"

[*He mimes the MOTHER, leaning over the balcony and shouting.*]

"Palestine! Make my boy's cat fly at once! If you don't, I'm coming down, and I'll nail you up!"

[*He mimes JESUS looking at the palms of his hands, a bit worried.*]

"Alright, line up all your birds."

"He's breathing on them! There they go!" [*He mimes the staggering flight of the sundry birds.*] Whoosh... The peacock. Quack, quack... Whoosh... the sausage. Chirp, chirp... whoosh! The tart. Tweet, tweet... Vrrrm.. the big turd. Clunk, clunk, whoomf... The cat! Whoosh... Miaow... Yum, yum, yum! The cat ate all the birds in the sky!

"Oh! That's great! I've never seen anything so funny...!"

"Let's have some more birds. Come on, all together!"

And everybody started making birds. Even children from other parts of town started arriving. The whole square was full of children making little clay models. Birds of every shape and size. They were playing, laughing and singing!

But at that moment, whammo! The big door on the square swings open. And out comes a black horse, a handsome animal, all decked out, and ridden by a little boy, all shiny-faced, with bright eyes and his hair properly combed... feathers in his hat, dressed in silk and velvet, with a lace collar. And he was surrounded by soldiers in armour, and they too had feathers in their hats, and were riding white horses.

That little boy was the son of the lord of the whole city.

[*He mimes the little boy looking down from his horse and asking the local kids:*]

"Hey, children, what are you playing at?"

"Ignore him. He's just a troublemaker. He's the son of the Lord of the Manor. Ignore him, Palestine. Make out you haven't noticed him. Pretend he's not there."

"Won't you tell me what you're playing? Can I play too?"

"No!"

"And why not, pray?"

"Because... Because every time we want to play with you, rich man's son, you say no! And because every time we come to your house where you've got your horses and lots of big toys, you get your guards to chase us away. Well now we've got a lovely game, the best game in the world, but Palestine is in charge of our game, and he belongs to us. You might be rich, but you haven't got Palestine. Palestine's on our side. Isn't that right, Palestine? Splosh, splosh!" [*He mimes kissing Jesus.*] "Don't go off with the rich boy, eh? Don't be a Judas, will you?!"

"But may I know what this game is?"

"Easy-peasy... We're making birds. Then Palestine breathes on them, and makes them fly. Would you like to play too?"

"Oh yes."

"Alright then, pull out your willy, blow on it, and let's see if you can make *that* fly!"

[*He mimes a great guffaw of laughter.*]

The rich man's son was absolutely furious! Eyes bulging out of his head. Black with anger. He took a spear from one of his soldiers and spurred his horse. The horse rode in among the children, and the boy started shouting like a madman:

"If I can't play, then none of you are going to play either!"

Crunch, crunch... With the hooves of his horse he smashed all the little clay figures. There they were, all over the ground, shattered into little bits. The children started crying... and throwing lumps of clay at him... and the soldiers arrived on their horses, and began shouting:

"Scram! Get out of here, get out, go on! Because he's allowed to do anything he wants, because he's the rich man's son!"

All the mothers looked out of their windows.

"That's naughty! That was such a good game! Didn't cost anything... Our children were happy, and you..."

And the soldiers:

"Scram, mothers! Get out of the way, because you'll wind up on the end of a spear if you don't!"

Slam, crash, bang, bang! All the windows closed. All the doors closed. The square emptied. The only people left were the little boy, the rich man's son, on his black horse, and his soldiers, who were laughing. And nobody noticed that Baby Jesus was still there, near the fountain. With eyes wide open, full of tears... And he was looking at the sky, which had filled up with clouds.

[*He mimes the little boy, turning to heaven and shouting.*]

"Daaaad, Daaad!"
The clouds opened: Creeeak, vrooom, vraaam!

[*He mimes the clouds opening up, and GOD peering out from between them.*]

"What's the matter?"

[*He imitates the tone of a little boy trying to hold back the tears.*]

"Dad, it's me, Jesus..."
"What happened, son?"
"Sob, sob, sob... That boy's naughty, he broke all the little clay things that we made to play with. He scrunched them all up with his horse. Sob, sob, sob, sob..."

[*He cries, sobbing.*]

"Look, son, was it really necessary to give your father a fright for such a silly thing? I was all the way on the other side of the universe, and I had to come tearing across... I punctured twelve clouds, not to mention running down a dozen cherubim, and my halo's all over the place – it'll take an eternity to get it right again!"
"Yes, but he's been naughty. He's the rich man's son. He's got everything! He's got all sorts of toys, but when he saw that we were enjoying ourselves, he... sob, sob, sob... [*He sobs.*]... he broke everything... Waaaah... [*He cries.*] And I tried so hard..."
"Speak up, son."
"And I tried so hard to do the miracle, to get the birds to fly, so's I could have some friends to play with... And it was nice, because we all made friends... but now I'm all on my own again like before. All my friends have run away... Waaaah! [*He cries.*] I'm ever so unhappy, Dad, ever so... Waaaah!"
"You're right. I have to say that smashing up children's games, destroying their dreams, really is the worst of

violence... But he's just a kid, son... What do you expect me to do, eh?"

[*JESUS lets out a long, thoughtful, weeping sigh, and then says, in a very matter-of-fact tone:*]

"Kill him!" [*He smiles, looking heavenwards, naughtily.*] "Eh?"

[*He mimes smiles and little shrugs aimed at convincing his father.*]

"But Son, I sent you down from heaven specially to teach peace between men, and to speak to them of love. The first time someone upsets you, you want to kill them?! That's not a very good start, is it, eh?!"

"Is that asking too much? Well, alright then, cripple him... Blind him, eh? Or blind him *and* cripple him!"

"No, you can't do that sort of thing, son. You can't just go being violent to people."

"You can't eh? What you mean is, *you* can't? Can *I* kill him, then?"

"Alright then, do what you like. I can see there's no point my talking to you. But don't go round telling people it was me that did it."

Creak, vraaam, the clouds disappeared... The clouds faded away, and once again the sky was clear. And time had stood still. Once again, there was the rich man's son, laughing, and the soldiers sniggering, and Baby Jesus nearby, calling out:

"Cooee...! Rich man's son!"

"Eh?"

"Tee-hee-hee."

[*He laughs the sly laugh of somebody preparing a wicked joke.*]

"So, you're laughing, eh? You've created all this mess around here, you've smashed all our little birds, broken up our game. And there you are, pleased as Punch, thinking that nobody in the whole world can touch you. Not even your father, eh? Well, how would it be if I decided to get you struck by lightning, eh? You're laughing? Don't you believe me?"

Vroooonch! A terrible lightning bolt flashed from the eyes of Baby Jesus. [*He mimes the terrible flash of fire.*] A tongue of fire, like a snake on fire, twined itself all round the boy, picked him up, turned him over, threw him to the ground, and he turned into terracotta as if he'd been made in an oven. Blam! All smoking!!

And all the women looking out from their balconies started shouting:

"What is this terrible thing that you've done?"

The soldiers went white as sheets and galloped off on their horses.

The Madonna had heard all the shouting and came running:

"What's happened? What have you done, son?"

"Nothing... Just done a miracle. My first miracle. Look, he's still warm."

"But what... It's a little boy? It's a little boy that you've turned into terracotta!! But what have you done? What is this? Why?"

"Well, he was nasty to me, Mum!"

"I don't want to hear another word! Bring him back to life at once!"

"No." [*In a whining tone of voice.*]

"Jesus, do as I say! Think of this boy's poor mother... She'll have a fit...! bring him back to life at once...!"

"But I don't know how to, Mum. I only learned how to do lightning bolts, and I haven't learnt the bit about how to bring them back to life!"

"Don't tell fibs. Bring him back to life, and get on with it! Don't you realise that if the soldiers come, we're going to have to run away again... And your father, and I have just found work!"

"Alright, but... You know, you can't just do a miracle and then undo it at once! Alright then, I will bring him back to life. But I'll do it with a kick..."

Blam! A big kick up his clay bum... Vrooom... The little boy turns back to flesh and blood, brought back to life.

He stands there, scared, holding his bum with his hands and looking around him:

"What happened, what was that, what's going on?!"

And Baby Jesus answered:

"It was me... A miracle... Struck you by lightning... Then brought you back to life! That's 'cos my Mum came... So you'd best thank the Holy Mother! You still feel your bum smarting from the kick, eh...? Well, remember that, because it's an allegory! Very instructive for everyone who took fright and ran off and hid behind their shutters..."

[*He points to the windows all around the square.*]

"Because the day that they start to think for themselves, then you'd better watch out... because you're going to get *such* a kicking! Your bum will swell, and swell, and swell, and swell, until blam! It'll burst! And there you'll be, for all eternity without an arsehole! Amen!"

THE END